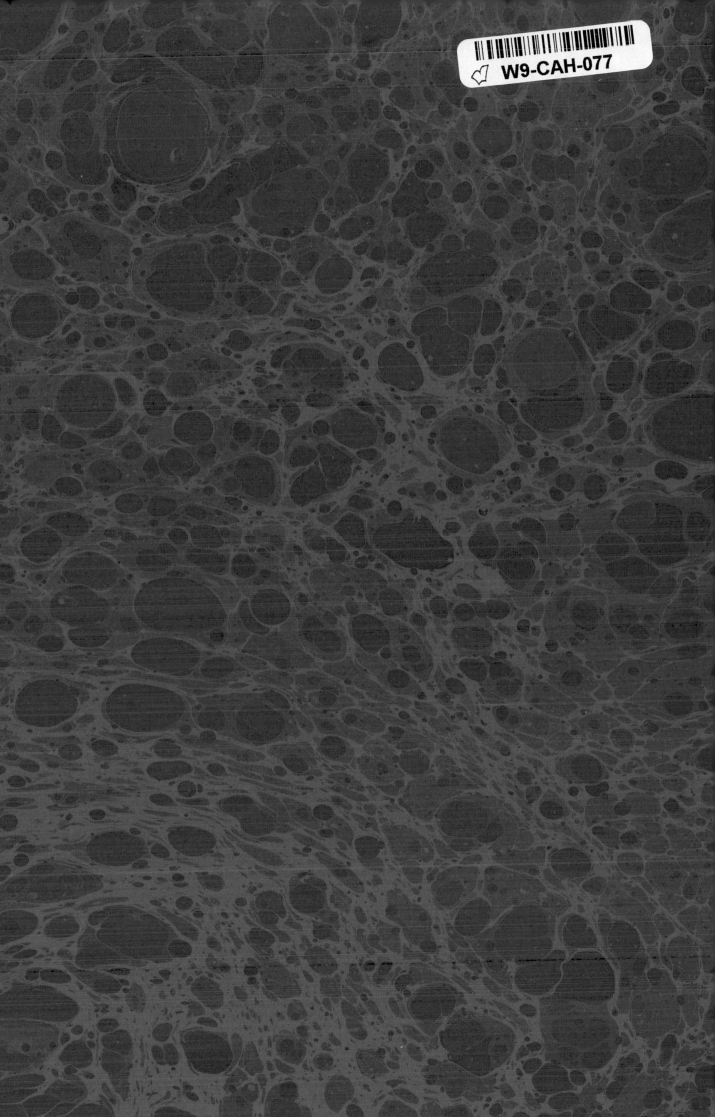

The Enchanted World

THE FALL OF CAMELOT

The Enchanted World

THE FALL OF CAMELOT

by the Editors of Time-Life Books

Time-Life Books • Alexandria, Virginia

THE CONTENT

PROLOGUE

Three ships set sail once from the stony coast of Wales, three low, square-sailed ships running before an easterly wind. Above their decks, the spears of warriors glittered in bristling array; among the spear blades, the warriors' standards snapped and fluttered, and the painted lions, leopards, wolves and griffins that adorned them danced in the sun. On the lead ship, one banner rose higher than the rest, displaying thirteen golden crowns on a field of blue. This was the standard of Arthur, High King of Britain. The crowns signified his own royalty and that of the twelve petty kingdoms that the young King had brought under his rule, but Arthur was after greater prey than these. Arrogant in his quick-won glory, he sought to invade Annwfn, the world of Faerie, and take its magic treasure for his own. This was a raiding party.

It was a mighty company, high in spirit and strong in arms—and in more than arms: On the King's ship sailed the Welsh bard Taliesin. Bards often accompanied kings to war. The poets sang men into battle and, later, in their songs, preserved those men's deeds for history. But Taliesin was more than a bard. He was an enchanter, a man who could take the shape of a lantern or an eagle or a harpstring. In his youth he had slain dragons, and he had sung at battles where the very trees pulled up their roots and marched heavily across the ground to join the fray. The old man's presence on the venture was a safeguard, for even the people of Annwfn gave reverence to the powers of Taliesin.

Another safeguard sailed with Arthur: The mightiest warrior in the world was in his company. Taliesin named this man Llwch Lleminawc, which meant in Welsh "the fated one," but Taliesin did not say what the epithet might portend, and no later chroniclers spoke of him.

In fact, everything the bard recorded of the venture was wrapped in mystery; and when the words of his song were written down, they seemed to glow and fade on the page, revealing and concealing meaning. Arthur sailed west across the sea, beyond the shore of the world, recounted the enchanter. The King's ships beached on a mist-shrouded island where a fortress rose, tower upon tower, hall upon hall, battlement upon battlement of translucent glass, shimmering in the light of the place, which was now twilight, now night-dark.

In that strange hour, the warriors passed a sentinel who would not speak, and they found the wonders they had come to find: a wellspring of wine bubbling from the ground and a caldron rimmed with pearls, infinitely precious. Nine maidens guarded this caldron, for it was a vessel of magic, giants' work charged with the powers of the first world. Its blue-enameled sides gave forth a radiance that endowed good men with the wisdom to sing and the courage to fight. And the caldron provided meat for brave men only; it would not cook the food of cowards.

Arthur and his warriors stole the caldron; they carried it away and hid it, safe in their own territory. But they paid heavily for the treasure they took.

The lesser payment was in life. Six thousand warriors of Annwfn defended the glass fortress and the caldron against the human invaders. Although Taliesin did not describe the battle—except to praise the valor of the knight Llwch Lleminawc—he told its grim results. Only a handful of the company returned alive to Britain. "When we went with Arthur in his splendid labors, Arthur of mournful memory," sang the bard, "save seven, none returned from the enclosure of the perfect ones, the enclosure resting on the height."

The greater payment was lifelong, which perhaps was why Taliesin cloaked his chronicle in shadowy phrases and why Arthur never afterward spoke of his adventure or showed the treasure he had won. It was a terrible thing to challenge the ancient powers of the other world; it was a foolhardy act to steal a relic of old magic from the place where it rightly dwelled.

The bard, it seemed, understood the danger, for in his oblique fashion, he included warnings in his account of the venture—warnings that Arthur understood only when it was too late. Taliesin said that amid the splendors of Annwfn's fortress of glass a prison tower rose; in that tower, bound with chains of steel, a mortal king was kept, a man whose ceaseless lamentations could be heard throughout the fairy island. His name was Gweir. He had, it seemed, offended the old ones and thus brought perpetual imprisonment upon himself and famine upon his country. And, said Taliesin, the long-vanished Kings Pwyll and Pryderi served in Annwfn. Father and son, the two had ruled the kingdom of Dyfed in Wales before Arthur's time; their trespasses on the lands of Faerie had brought a wasting enchantment to their domain.

These prisoners of Annwfn had reigned in an era when humankind seemed more vulnerable and the princes of Faerie wandered freely on the earth. Arthur was the lord of a new age. The star of human power, he gathered the realms of Britain into his hands. Even Arthur, however, could not safely insult the hidden elder world that was not human. The Princes of Annwfn took vengeance for the loss of their treasure. Their eyes were keen, their reach long, their weapons many, their patience infinite. They sent their servants among the conquering mortals, servants who worked in secret ways, who formed with threads of shadow the cracks that caused the British King's bright honor to crumble into dust and ruin to settle on his dominion.

I

↬ ARTHUR ↬

ighty indeed was Tintagel, fortress of the Dukes of Cornwall, looming on a slate-cliffed headland high above the sea. No army could breach its defenses. Yet on a winter's night between one year and the next, a frail creature, no more than half a man, stole away with the castle's treasure and took it into his own keeping.

His was a deed of masterly stealth, a blend of both quickness and patience. In the depths of the night, he flitted across the narrow isthmus that linked Tintagel to the Cornish coast. With his black cloak gathered about him, he was a shadow among shadows, a mere stirring in the air. Guards paced the battlements above but they did not detect his approach, nor did they hear his light footsteps on the rain-slick stone. Then the intruder vanished into an archway marking a hidden postern gate that faced westward across the sea.

Motionless, he waited through the small hours. The rain ceased after a time, and the cold night wind died. Above the castle towers, the ordered stars – the Crown, the Dragon, the Archer, the Huntsman with his dogs, the sisters of the Pleiades – appeared and pursued the stately figures of their dance, then faded as dawn approached. Abruptly, the door in the wall swung open; a young woman was there, holding in her arms a swaddled infant. Without a word, she gave it to the watcher; without a word, he received it into the black folds of his cloak. Then he turned back onto the cliff, sped silently through the morning light, and disappeared.

Thus was the infant Arthur, heir to Britain, placed under a shield of magic, not to be seen again for fifteen years. Merlin the Enchanter was the man who took him from the fortress where his mother lay. Merlin was the man who hid him.

Merlin, that enigmatic being, son of a human woman and a creature of the other world, prophet and magician, had brought about the infant's birth. The boy's father was Uther Pendragon – Uther the Chief of Warriors, in Welsh – who ruled a troubled realm, a Britain torn by the internal strife of loosely united petty kingdoms and menaced from without by the greed and savagery of Saxon hordes from the European mainland. Uther had conceived a passion for the wife of one of his own Dukes.

↬ ↬ ↬ ↬ ↬ ↬ ↬ ↬ ↬ ↬ ↬ ↬ ↬ ↬ ↬ ↬

*A headland fortress called Tintagel
was the birthplace of Arthur of Britain. Here, safe from
assault, laired the Dukes of Cornwall.*

Igraine, the Duchess of Gorlois of Cornwall, was the woman; Gorlois sequestered her at Tintagel, where Uther could not reach her. Maddened, the King turned to magic. He summoned Merlin.

And Merlin gave Uther what he wished; he waited until Gorlois was gone from Tintagel, defending his eastern territories. Then, by enchantment, the old man changed Uther's shape to that of the Cornish Duke; in this form, the King was admitted one night to Tintagel and had his will.

Merlin demanded a price for the pandering: The price was any child born of that night's union. Uther shrugged and agreed, and he had to keep his word, although he named Igraine his Queen when Gorlois died in battle, making the infant she carried in her womb his rightful heir.

So even before Arthur's life began, the eyes of the other world turned toward him. Uther's passion was a force that rent the fabric of human honor and human order; it left a path where the old ones might enter the mortal world. And Merlin, who aided the King and guarded the child of the King's desire, was half of the fairy race himself, a living link to the magic of the older age.

Why the Enchanter wanted the child the chroniclers never told; doubtless they did not know, for Merlin kept his own counsel. Some thought he hid Arthur for the child's safety while the British warred among themselves; some said that the old blood flowing in his veins made him treasure his power as kingmaker in the human world.

In any case, kingmaker he was, although none would know it for some time to come. The infant Arthur disappeared into the mountain fastness of Wales, placed in the care, it was said, of a lord named Ector. Merlin periodically appeared in Uther's court, watching Igraine and the King, keeping guard over the succession. He saw Igraine's three daughters by Gorlois—fey, witchlike maidens, adept, it was whispered, with the tools of enchantment—safely married to minor princes and sent away from court. Morgause, the eldest, became the Queen of Lot of Lothian and Orkney, a harsh, hotheaded lord who held almost unrivaled power in the north. Elaine married King Nentres of Garlot and faded out of history. The youngest daughter, Morgan, became the wife of Urien of Gorre. Those were all the children of Igraine; except for Arthur, she bore no others.

Therefore, when Merlin knew that Uther was dying—after the King's last battle against invaders from the north, when he led his army from a litter, being too weak to sit a horse—he went to the King and asked for the word he wanted: That Arthur, Uther's only son, should be made King of the Britons. And, said the chroniclers, Uther assented. That was two years after Arthur's birth.

Thirteen years more passed before Merlin made the move to place Arthur on the throne—thirteen long years while the princes of Britain fought and the people suffered, thirteen years while the child, who did not know he was a king, grew to young manhood. Arthur underwent hard and patient training during this period, and when he at last appeared, he was royal indeed, the very prince and flower of chivalry.

His existence was revealed to the world at Christmastide. In the weeks and months beforehand, Merlin's messengers rode throughout Britain, summoning the princes of the realm to London to take counsel about the crowning of a king who would unite them once again, as they had been under Uther. All through December, parties of horsemen wound along the dirt tracks and crumbling highways that led to the city. Outside the walls, a great encampment grew on the high heaths and frosted stubble of the winter fields, a sprawl of bright tents and gilded standards, all overhung by a haze of smoke from cooking fires.

Old magic slipped past the defenses of Tintagel. Merlin the Enchanter carried away the infant Arthur and placed him in hiding.

An ancient sword embedded in a sacred stone gave proof that Arthur
was High King of Britain. Many sought to extract the weapon, but only he succeeded.

And within the walls of London, where Merlin walked the narrow streets in his somber scholar's gown, enchantment was at work. At the city's heart, close by the square tower that was its ancient fortress, a chapel stood. The chapel was a small one, built to cover some old god's shrine; a cloister and grassy courtyard adjoined it, reminders that it had once been attached to a monastery. In the yard a massive stone appeared, pierced by a broadsword. On the stone, in letters that gave their own light, was a legend: *Whoso pulleth this sword from this stone is rightfully born King of all England.*

All the Kings—Lot, Urien of Gorre, Ban of Benwic in France, Idres of Cornwall and many others—came to study the sword. Its import was clear to them, for they were descended from sword-bearing warrior tribes and from lords whose emblems of office were sacred stones. The coronation seat of the Irish King, for instance, was the Lia Fail—the Stone of Destiny. It shrieked when the rightful King's foot touched it. All the British Kings therefore tried the sword: Who knew which blood would plumb the magic? But the stone would not yield its treasure to them.

Merlin observed the trials without comment. But on the first day of Christmas, when the Kings gathered in the fortress hall, he called them to silence. In his cold, dry voice Merlin said, "He is not yet here who shall achieve the sword." Then he left them to speculate, to form and break alliances, to plot among themselves.

So Christmas passed in mutterings and quarrels among the factions jockeying for power. The new year came, and with it bright sunlight and an icy wind that swept through the twisting streets of London, rattling the shutters of the houses and the painted signboards of the shops.

Under one of those boards—a painted bush, signifying a wineshop—three men stood on New Year's morning. Two of them were short of stature, compact and dark in the manner of the Welsh. Both were armored in mail; they held their helmets under their arms as they talked in the singing accents of the west. The third man was tall and broad of shoulder, with red-gold hair that lifted in the wind. So strong was he, so easy in his grace, that he seemed to catch and hold the sunlight, and although he wore the tunic and cloak of a squire, he drew the eyes of the passersby. He leaned against the wineshop wall, oblivious to the admiring coos of the good-wives, and listened to his companions. The golden man was Arthur, a fine lordling not yet old enough, it seemed, for knighthood. The other two were Kay, whom he thought to be his elder brother, and Ector, his supposed father. All of them were newly arrived from Ector's Welsh lands.

Kay, always short-tempered, was in a foul humor. He had left his sword at the camp outside the city walls. Ector's rough comments on his carelessness enraged the younger man. Unwilling—and unable—to quarrel with his father, he turned on Arthur and ordered him to fetch the sword.

Arthur, tired of talk and glad of action, answered Kay with a jaunty half salute and strode off down the street between the leaning, timbered houses, weaving his way among the frozen puddles, the pigs that rooted in refuse, the fishwives with their heavy baskets, the bakers with their stacks of great round loaves. At the bottom of the path, an elderly man plucked at his sleeve. The golden head bent for a moment, giving courteous attention. Then, with the old man pacing at his side, Arthur turned a corner and vanished from view.

When he returned an hour later, his face was drawn and grave, but his eyes were bright. In his hand he held an unsheathed broadsword. He raised his brows inquiringly when he saw his brother standing alone. Kay gestured toward the wineshop, where Ector had gone. Then he held out his hands for the sword. Arthur laid the blade gently across Kay's hands, saying as he did so, "This sword is mine, brother."

Kay turned the sword over, examining the filigree that ornamented the hilt and the agates and carnelians that gleamed among the gold. He said, "This is not a sword of ours. Whose is it?"

"In a churchyard beside the fortress there stands a stone," said Arthur. "This sword was in the stone. I called the sword forth as I was told, and it came into my hand."

Kay stared at him with narrowed eyes. "I am the elder," he said. Then he shouted for his father, whose face appeared in the shop window.

"Sir," said Kay, "this is the sword from the sacred stone that we have heard of. I have found it; it brings me a crown." Arthur made a sharp movement, swiftly checked. Ector's face disappeared from the window. In a moment, he was with them.

The old man looked without expression at his sons, the one blazing with white fury, the other defiant, but trembling enough so that the jewels in the sword he held winked in the light. "Let us go, then, to the place of the stone," said Ector.

They did that, and when they stood in the quiet courtyard beside the empty stone, Ector turned to Kay. "Son," he said, "swear now on your honor that you yourself found the sword you hold and drew it from the stone."

The very walls of the yard seemed to breathe and listen. Finally, Kay shook his head. "I lied," he said. "My brother Arthur found the stone and drew the sword from it." And he returned the sword to Arthur.

L et us see, then," said Ector. At his gesture, Arthur replaced the sword in the great stone. Ector tried it; the hilt burned in his hand, he said, but the sword did not move. Kay tried, but the weapon remained fast in its prison. At last, Arthur put his hands to the golden hilt. The letters on the stone blazed out; with a metallic hiss, the sword slid free.

Ector sank slowly to his knees. He placed his hands over Arthur's on the sword hilt and began the solemn words of the oath of fealty. As he did so, Kay knelt beside him.

"Father," said Arthur, when Ector had finished, "do not kneel."

"Nay, lord, I am not your father but only he who fostered and trained you. I knew well that you were of higher blood than mine."

"That is true," said another voice. A face glimmered in the shadow of the cloister. Then Merlin came forth.

"You are he who brought me the boy to care for," said Ector.

"You are he who guided me to this stone," said Arthur.

"I am," replied the Enchanter. "I am he who has brought you to the throne, son of Uther Pendragon, High King of Britain."

Arthur's head went up; his hand tightened on the hilt of the sword as the mantle of power gathered around him, and his voice was clear when he claimed the crown.

The claim was not welcome everywhere, for the lords of Britain had no wish to be governed by a stranger. But they had the word of the Enchanter that Arthur was the rightful King and, what mattered more, they had the evidence of the sword and the evidence of the man himself.

The blood of kings ran in Arthur's veins, and he had been schooled for a high place. Within a year, therefore, he was crowned, and the princes of the land had bent the knee to him. Those who, years before, had loved Uther — Baudwin of Britain, Ulfin, Brastias, Leodegran of Camelerd, Pellinore of the Isles — came willingly, bringing their armies. Many more, however, were secret enemies, waiting for the chance to seize the throne. Chief among these was Lot, brooding in the north, on his windswept islands.

He struck first a year after the coronation, when Arthur held court at the fortress of Caerleon in Wales. To that assembly rode Lot with the allies he had gathered: Urien of Gorre, Nentres of Garlot, the King of Scotland, the King of Carados. When Arthur's messenger greeted them, they sent back word, as the chroniclers wrote, that "it was a great shame to all of them to see such a boy have the rule of so noble a realm."

The first response came from Merlin. He stepped one night, first a shadow and then a solid man, from the campfire where the rebel Kings had gathered. He surveyed them with wintry eyes, the kingmaker serving the King he had made.

"You would do better to give over this folly, lords. You would not prevail, not if you were ten times as many."

Urien, suddenly afraid, made the sign against evil. Lot spat at Merlin's feet. "Are we well advised to listen to a dream reader?" he said, and he laughed.

But the Enchanter had faded again into the flames.

The next morning, Arthur descended on the camp with his cavalry. Golden crowns gleamed on his shield, and a dreadful sword glittered in his hands — not the sword of ceremony that had made him King, but an elf-made sword, the weapon Caliburn, drawn from a lake by Merlin's magic. No enemy could withstand it. Moreover, even its sheath was magic: A touch of its scabbard, warriors whispered, could heal the gravest wound. It was no sword for mortal men, they said.

In the battle that followed, the King stayed always to the fore, and the great sword killed and killed. Lot's infantry was trampled; the rebel Kings and their knights

Unfathomable was the mystery of Merlin. In his veins ran fairy blood, yet he guarded a mortal king.

held formation but were driven steadily back by the High King's wolfish fury. At the last, they turned and fled.

Arthur pursued them—but much later. For months he waited, weighing the reports that came down from the Scottish territories, reports of a gathering of eleven armies under Lot, a host that would sweep across England to bring the High King down.

Before Lot could move, however, Arthur was on the march. Along the northern track his battle train moved—knights and squires, foot soldiers, pack mules, supply wagons, armorers, surgeons and straggling women. They traveled through heavily wooded country, and all along the edges of the track the trees stirred and rustled, seeming to offer a faint echo to the slapping and jingling of harnesses, the creaking of wagon wheels, the clatter of bows, the thud of marching feet. But these were no echoes. Merlin had made an alliance with Ban of Benwic and Bors of Gaul; he had cast a cloak of invisibility over the French Kings' armies, and he himself led them north, through the forest, a shadow host flanking the armies of the High King.

The ghostly army turned the tide for Arthur in the end. Ban and Bors could not in honor keep themselves shielded with invisibility; they could, however, remain in ambush so that Lot's armies were drawn forward, tempted by Arthur's seemingly small force. And that is what happened. The armies met on a field at the borders of the forest of Bedegraine, hard by a river that marked the Scottish border. There, Arthur and his knights waited, still as stones on their mighty horses, their lances resting on their thighs. Lot and his eleven Kings charged, screaming. And then death's cold hand touched man and beast so wantonly that, according to the chroniclers, the horses were soon up to their fetlocks in blood and the device on Arthur's shield could not be seen for the gore that bespattered it. When the fray was at its worst, Ban and Bors and their companies slipped out from the trees. Lot and his men checked at the sight of this host, led by two Kings who were called the best warriors in the world. Their spirit failed them then. Stumbling over broken bodies and through pools of blood, they fled from the field of battle.

Arthur pressed forward, his heralds beside him, Bors and Ban just behind. But the horses halted of their own accord and stood sweating

✄ ✄ ✄ ✄ ✄ ✄ ✄ ✄ ✄

and trembling. No spur could move them. Merlin stood on the field. "It is enough killing," said the Enchanter. "You have slain three quarters of their men. You will not follow now; you will have other opportunity. And enemies are on the northern shores. Lot must secure his rear before he threatens English kingdoms."

Merlin said no more, but all who listened knew the rightness of his words. The High King withdrew into his own lands. His under Kings dispersed to their various territories, all save Bors and Ban, his allies from across the water.

The three Kings repaired to Arthur's rough fortress, called, like the forest that surrounded it, Bedegraine, to be greeted by messengers from his ally Leodegran of Camelerd, in the southwest of England, near Cornwall. Merlin stood beside the High King as the heralds spoke urgently of the enemies of Leodegran, men who sought to overthrow the kingdom. The Enchanter studied the men intently, then frowned.

"Lord," said the Enchanter, who could always see the pattern of Arthur's life, "do not go to Leodegran."

"Enchanter, do not seek to bind me longer. Leodegran was my father's vassal and is my own ally as well," the King replied. He left the hall.

So the High King rode south in the autumn, through the water meadows and marshes called the Summer Country, home of folk who lived their lives on small and shifting lake villages and had leather boats for horses. These people were the isolated survivors of an early age; their metal was bronze, not iron, and they worshipped old gods strange to Arthur and his men. He passed the high hill ruled by Melwas, a prince known to court the old ones; the hill was covered with apple trees heavy with crimson fruit, but no mortal man dared touch those apples. They were the food of Faerie, the soldiers said.

Down to the coast Arthur's army marched, then along the shore to the fortress of Leodegran. He fought like a lion for Leodegran, and won.

Chroniclers say that ten thousand men died in the battle, but that seems unlikely: The world was sparsely populated, and military actions were matters of hundreds, not thousands.

❧ ❧ ❧ ❧ ❧ ❧ ❧ ❧ ❧

From a high window gazed Guinevere, daughter of Leodegran of Camelerd, a princess fit in truth to be a queen. Arthur saw her there, and the image lingered long and fair in his memory.

Yet victory was not the prize of Camelerd. After the fighting, when the High King feasted in his vassal's hall, the wheel of his fate began to turn. The hall was a high one, hung with fine weaving; long tables lined it. The lord's own table was vast and round, not like the trestles used by other kings. The vessels that adorned it were of glass and gold, reflecting the light of torches and hearth.

And the maiden who served the wine of the High King reflected the light as well. She was a tall girl; her hair hung unbound and unornamented except for a princess's circlet, and the hair was the brown of autumn leaves, touched with gold from the sun. Her eyes were downcast as befitted a maiden; the lashes made shadows on her flesh. The robe she wore was white; the hands that held the drinking horn were long and pale; she had a scent of flowers about her.

Arthur was no stranger to women: He was the High King, a golden warrior unrivaled on the field, and he had their admiration. He had a son already by a knight's daughter named Lionors, who had once attracted him. But this woman clearly was no mere knight's child; and far from showing admiration, she had neither glanced nor spoken. He was charmed.

Leodegran, on Arthur's right, caught the High King's look and said, "That is my daughter, lord."

"A noble maiden," replied the King. He turned to speak to her, but the girl had gone from the hall.

"Her name is Guinevere," said Leodegran, then guided the talk to other matters.

Arthur saw no more of Leodegran's daughter until the day he left the King's fortress. As he mounted, a movement caught his eye. With the warrior's quick attention, he turned in the saddle. The maiden stood in a window of a low stone tower, gazing gravely at him. He lifted a hand in farewell; then he rode away.

❧ ❧ ❧ ❧ ❧ ❧ ❧ ❧ ❧ ❧ ❧ ❧ ❧ ❧ ❧

II

❧ MORGAUSE ❧

From the battlements of Caerleon, high on a spur of rock above the River Usk, stirrings in Arthur's territory could be detected at great distance. Along the valley track that cut from the coast of Wales to its heart, royal parties, bright in silks and gold, came to pay tribute to the High King. Heralds rode hither and thither on Arthur's business. And many lesser folk moved through the valley: shepherds driving their flocks toward the mountains; wandering friars in dun-colored robes; merchants bound for trade fairs, grouped for safety in long caravans of heavy-laden wagons. The sentries called these everyday travelers *pieds poudreux* – dusty feet – and gave them no more than idle glances, for they posed no threat to the High King's peace. But that peace was more vulnerable than they knew, and the road would bring its undoing. In its varied traffic one clear August day was a woman who served the forces that determined Arthur's fate.

Her party was a small one. Two heralds preceded her, one bearing a standard blazoned with a double eagle, one carrying the white flag of truce. The woman herself rode astride a black horse; she was straight-backed and slender, and the golden circlet of royalty adorned her dark hair. Behind her, flanked by a small guard and followed by a string of pack mules, rode four squires, all of them young, and one so modest in years that his mount was only a shaggy pony.

The crown and the standard told the story: The woman was the Queen of Lothian and Orkney; the white flag meant that either she or her husband sought Arthur's protection. On the walls of Caerleon, the sentries called to their officers, and by the time her little party had wound its way up the hill to the fortress, the gates stood open in welcome. Kay, the High King's foster brother, awaited them, the keys embossed on his signet indicating his office as Arthur's seneschal.

At a little distance from the gate, the Queen reined in her horse. Her heralds rode forward; they halted before Kay, and the standard bearer said, "Morgause of Lothian and Orkney greets the High King and craves audience with him. She bears messages from Lot, her husband."

"The High King sits in his hall," Kay replied. "She may attend him there." Mor-

Fierce and vigilant, a double eagle formed the crest of Lot of Lothian and Orkney.

gause raised her brows at this brusqueness, but she said nothing. She set her horse forward at a stately walk, gesturing to her companions, and the little company passed into Caerleon. They followed Kay across the grassy castle yard, with its long tilting field where the quintain used for practice hung idle in the noon heat; past archery butts; past barracks and armories; past kennels and stables and mews, all of them built into the fortress's inner curtain wall. The place was busy with animals and people. White-wimpled serving-women gossiped at a well, under the eyes of lounging soldiers; a smith stood sweating at the door of his forge, framed by the fireglow within. A lymerer passed with a pair of leashed hounds; squires held horses ready for their masters. They regarded Morgause without interest. They were used to supplicants.

At the door of the King's hall, Kay paused and said, "No foreign guard may enter. You go to the King alone, lady." The stammer that flawed his speech was prominent.

Morgause looked down at him from long, green eyes. She shook her head. "I will leave the house guard and the heralds, although my honor is due them. But my sons will stay by me." She held out a hand, and Kay, after a moment's hesitation, helped her to dismount. When she stood beside him, she added in a hissing whisper, "They say, Ector's son, that your speech was crippled by envy when the High King took your place at your mother's breast." And before the seneschal could reply, Morgause glided by him into Arthur's hall, followed by her sons.

In that cool and lofty chamber, where only thin shafts of sunlight broke the gloom, the Queen fell on her knees before the High King's throne, all arrogance

❧ ❧ ❧ ❧ ❧ ❧ ❧ ❧ ❧ ❧ ❧ ❧ ❧ ❧ ❧ ❧

masked and melted into softness. She begged forgiveness for her husband's rebellion; she offered a promise of his fealty. She asked that Arthur take her sons under his protection and train them for knighthood at his court. Behind her, the boys stared at the golden King and stood as still as stones while she gave their names — Gawain and Agravain, Gaheris and Gareth.

With the grace peculiar to him, Arthur raised the supplicant to her feet and accorded her the kiss of peace. The dark head tilted back on the long neck; Morgause held the King in her green gaze and gave a small, red-lipped smile.

The invitation was unmistakable. And Arthur was not displeased. He was, after all, a conqueror. Tales of his valor had already spread — of his vigor in battle, of his delight in adventure. What the Queen's smile offered seemed no more than his due.

So the High King took the wife of his old enemy for his mistress. Morgause and her sons rested at Caerleon for a month. But if the bedding was pleasant, the price was high. Terrible dreams haunted Arthur's sleep — dreams of serpents, of perverse, mis-shapen beasts whose screams were louder, said the chroniclers, than the baying of thirty hounds, whose stench was that of death. Morgause in that month grew rosy and sleek; Arthur acquired a strained and ashen look, as if he were wasting.

Kay the seneschal watched all this, sullen but unspeaking. He sent messengers in search of the High King's guardian — not heralds, but huntsmen and woodsmen, who knew the secret byways and retreats of Arthur's realms. Late one evening, a cool breeze arose and blew through the great hall; the torches flickered and blazed up, twisting the shadows of the company so that they danced grotesquely on the walls. Then one shadow was added to their number. It was that of the Enchanter. When the breeze died, the old man stood enfleshed, a bent figure by Arthur's chair. He scanned the King's gaunt face and that of the woman who sat by him at his table. "Well, lord?" was all he said. At that moment, Morgause laid her white hand on the High King's arm. As if drugged by his passion, he rose and left the hall with her, acknowledging Merlin by no more than an absent nod.

In the morning, however, he sought the Enchanter's chamber. He did not mention the woman. But he asked Merlin for ease from his dreams, and he freely told them.

erlin listened, his bony hands resting on his knees, his shadowed eyes contemplating the King. He remained still for some moments. Then he said, "I will tell you a tale. There lived once a princess who had some skill at magic, but not enough to give her all she wanted. She lusted for her brother, and there her spells availed her nothing, for he cast her off. Then she took for her bedmate a demon or, say some people, a man of Faerie. And when she was with child by this being, she told her people that the child was her brother's, got on her by force. The people had him chained and cut. They loosed packs of dogs on him, and the dogs tore at his flesh until he died.

"The woman's time came. In agony she brought forth a monster, a thing part

Fair indeed was Morgause, wife of Lot the rebel King. She came to Arthur to sue for truce in her husband's name, and she offered herself for the High King's pleasure.

Arthur took Morgause to be his paramour, but she gave him little joy. When he was with her, his dreams were haunted by serpents and dark images of death.

With the voice of prophecy, Merlin the Enchanter showed Arthur the meaning of his dreams: that Morgause was his sister, that the May child she would bear him would one day bring him to his death.

serpent, part lion, part leopard, part lascivious hare. Its cry was that of the dog packs that had devoured her brother's flesh.

"The princess, thus betrayed, was killed for her deed, but the beast she bore, no man could kill. It ran free, destroying the work of men." His strange story done, Merlin fell into abstracted silence.

"Well, then," said Arthur. "Unfold the meaning of the tale."

"The woman you lie with is half your sister. She is one of the three daughters Igraine of Cornwall bore before she became the Queen of Uther Pendragon. Each of the three has some skill that is more than mortal. But Morgause is the vessel chosen to hold the sword that will destroy you."

"What is the sword?"

"The son she will bear you. She carries him now. The people will call him the child from the sea, but he will be the beast that ravages the works of men. He will destroy you and, with you, all your knights."

"Who chose her as the vessel?"

"That I cannot say. Envious creatures, full of mischief, older far than I, my King. But in taking Lot's wife, you also chose. All men have a fate, and it is men who cause that fate to unfold."

"You did not warn me of this sister."

"I cannot always see clearly. I thought there was no need." Then Merlin, according to the chroniclers, added in his riddling way, "I may well be sorry also, for I shall die a shameful death, and you shall die a worshipful death."

ithout another word, the King strode from the chamber, heading for the tower where Morgause was housed. He found her room empty, stripped of the furs she had brought, cleared of tapestries and cushions. Her boys were gone from the barracks. "She took them away," said Kay the seneschal, when he was summoned. "Back to the empty islands where she belongs." But no sight of the Queen's party was seen on the valley road; no trace of her ships appeared in the Severn ports. It seemed that enchantment speeded her way and shielded her from the High King's wrath.

A time of waiting followed. The country was quiet. In the southwest, a castle slowly rose on a hill by a river. A thousand workmen—clerks, carpenters, smiths, quarriers, masons, carriers, barrowmen, pickmen—labored there. Although the Welsh bards claimed that Arthur had three principal courts—"Caerleon-on-Usk in Wales, Celliweg in Cornwall and Penrhyn Rhionydd in the North"—it was Camelot, this splendid fortress palace, built in the first years of his glory, that would live on in the minds of the chroniclers.

As for the High King, afflicted with the idle warrior's restlessness, prevented by the peace with Lot from pursuing Lot's wife, he went adventuring. The chronicles of the time are fragmented, mere shards of history, but they afford glimpses of his valor.

❧ ❧ ❧ ❧ ❧ ❧ ❧ ❧ ❧ ❧ ❧ ❧ ❧ ❧ ❧ ❧

One story tells of a rogue King, a giant man called Ryons of Norgales, whose habit it was to ornament, or purfle, the borders of his cloak with the beards of lords he had conquered. Ryons' boast—widely reported—was that he had already captured eleven beards and that Arthur's would be the twelfth. When a messenger told Arthur of this prediction, the High King commented that his beard was "full young to make a purfle of it." He added, "Before long Ryons shall do me homage on both his knees, or else he shall lose his head. Tell him I will have his head unless he does me homage." Then he set out after Ryons. According to some accounts, the High King and two of his knights waylaid the man and killed forty of his warriors. Ryons, rather than be slain himself, yielded to Arthur and offered allegiance.

The chronicles also speak of other-world enemies, among them a cat, pulled as a kitten from a lake in a fisherman's net and taken to his cottage as a pet. The animal grew to monstrous size as soon as it was given shelter. It tore the fisherman to pieces and fled to the mountains, where it laired in a cave and laid waste to the countryside. Hearing of these things, the High King sought out the beast, with Merlin for his companion. The Enchanter whistled the animal from its lair, and Arthur braced himself to take its charge on his spear. So enormous was the cat, however, that it broke the King's spear in two. Then Arthur, "with his sword in his right hand and his shield at his breast," fought for his life. The cat's claws tore through the shield, through the King's hauberk, piercing his shoulder. With a desperate swing of the great sword Caliburn, Arthur severed the forelegs, and still the beast fought, rearing on its hind legs and snatching at the King with its great teeth. But Arthur delivered the death blow at last, and it retreated on bloody stumps to the shelter of its cave.

It was said, too, that Arthur pressed beyond the boundaries of his territories, that he invaded the realms of the old ones and braved their magic. People said that he ventured to lands where the fortresses were made of glass and robbed those lands of their treasure, that he journeyed to countries where unicorns ruled. No one knew whether this was true. The records of the ventures were written in riddles, and the treasures—if any indeed had been won—were hidden away or lost.

ut all such encounters with magic were overshadowed by the dark enchantment that threatened the High King's life and people. On a day in late spring the year after Morgause had arrived at Caerleon, Merlin stood before Arthur in his hall and said, "My lord, the child I warned you of was born on the first day of May. I can see no more than that, for he is hidden from me. I cannot tell where he may be found."

The High King was not ready to let the old ones make a mockery of his power. He ordered that every male child in the realm born on the first day of May of that year should be delivered into his keeping. He did not say why. He did not have to: The power of the High King was absolute then.

The riders of the King, bearing on their surcoats his device of golden crowns, fanned out across Britain, hastening to every little kingdom—south to Lyonesse and Cornwall, into the Welsh lands of Gorre and Sugales and Norgales, to the island realms of the west. To Candebenet they rode, and Strangore, Northumberland and Garlot. And they traveled to Lothian and Orkney as well.

In the hamlets and villages, in the towns, on the manors great and small, in the castles of the princes, the scenes were the same. The High King's messengers would summon the people together and show his seal and read his command. Sometimes the mothers would deliver up their infant sons readily, believing perhaps that the King would give them good fortune. As for those who might disobey the command or fail to hear of it, Arthur's men were skillful questioners, and it took them little time to discover what boy babies had been born on May Day. When they learned of infants who had not been offered freely, they took them. In the night they strode into reed huts, into cottages of wattle and daub, into the small stone houses of the poorly wooded north, where even the sleeping benches were made of stone. They knocked aside angry parents and lifted the children from their wooden cradles or pallets of straw. The

Caliburn, the fairy sword, was the weapon of King Arthur. The flaming blade was invincible; the scabbard had the power to heal the cruelest wound.

babies were already bundled up, whether in bleached linens or in silk or in the coarse rags of the poor; people swaddled their infants tightly in those days, to keep their limbs straight. The messengers placed them gently in the hollows formed by the high pommels of their saddles and rode away, down the narrow dirt tracks that led from the villages or the stone highways left from earlier days, when Rome held the land, and disappeared from view.

At Caerleon, Merlin said to Arthur at last, "The son you made has been found among these you have gathered. He was put to nurse at a farm on an out-island. I can tell you no more than that; my sight does not show me which of the children is he."

❧ ❧ ❧ ❧ ❧ ❧ ❧ ❧ ❧ ❧ ❧ ❧ ❧ ❧ ❧ ❧ ❧

All male infants born in Britain on May Day were placed in a rudderless
boat and cast upon the cruel sea. Thus Arthur thought
to thwart the prophecy that a May-born child would slay him. But one
infant survived—the child that Arthur feared.

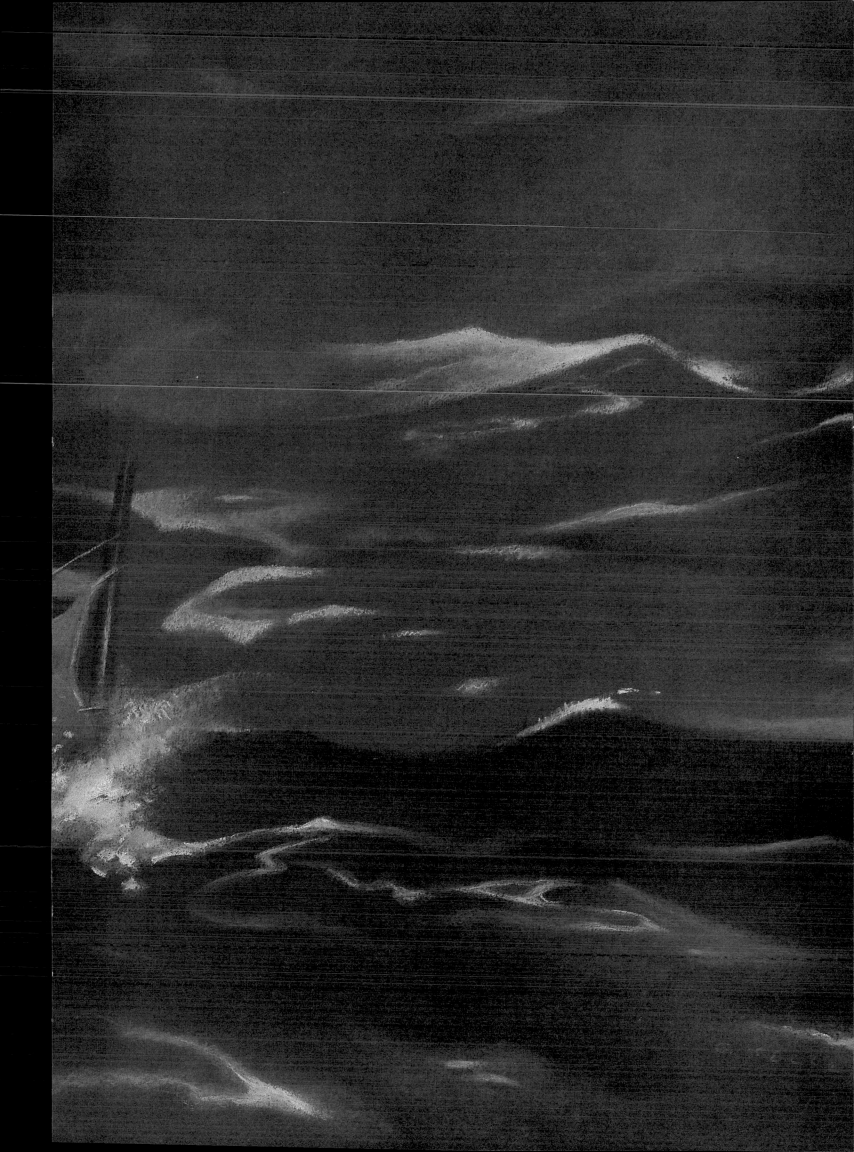

He paused, waiting for Arthur's response. When the King remained silent, he said, "Shall we then complete this work?" The High King nodded.

Lord and knights, farmers and fishermen, beggars and thieves, none of them knew where their infant sons had gone, and nothing was said to them. But after some months, whispers spread through the countryside, and they gave an ugly picture. They told of a stormy night when Arthur's soldiers carried the May babies to a seashore none could identify. They told how the children had been stripped of their swaddling and, naked, laid in a hide-covered ship. Its sail was set, and the ship was pushed off the shingle into the angry sea. As it sped wildly away from the shore, the soldiers turned and rode off. One watcher remained, however—a white-bearded man who stood by the water's edge, his robes rising like wings around him, until the wailing of the infants was lost in the storm and the ship disappeared in the sea spume.

It was Merlin who did the deed, the whisperers said, but Arthur who commanded that the deed be done.

But at Caerleon, after the whispers had spread, Merlin stared one autumn night into the hearth fire and said suddenly, "The child lives, lord. The sea gave it back; it thrives in some peasant's cottage, but where I cannot say."

Arthur's reply was strained and weary. "How can you tell?"

"I saw him for a moment in the flame; I heard his cry in the wind at the door."

"Those deaths are on my soul," said the High King. "And for nothing."

Merlin shrugged. "How many perished? Fewer than die in a siege or a sack. Fewer than would have starved. Fewer than the wasting sickness would have taken. Your race is a frail one."

This was the old Enchanter's only comment on the slaughter of the innocents. But its meaning was clear enough to those who knew the age. That Arthur was King had been shown by a sign from the gods, and something of divinity clung to his person. In him resided the safety of the kingdom: He was the sword that defended it and the font of its health; some believed that the very fertility of the land depended on his vigor. A threat to the King was therefore a threat to his entire realm, for if the King fell, strife and war, disease and famine would surely follow, destroying the fragile order that humankind imposed upon the world. It was clear enough to Merlin, from the circumstances of the child's conception and from the way its whereabouts were shielded from his vision, that the old ones were at work, clawing at the foundation of Arthur's power. In Merlin's terms, any weapon that could be used against them was justified, no matter how terrible that weapon might be.

The chroniclers, understandably, had little to say about the wicked deed; they simply recorded it without comment and passed on to other matters. No account of theirs, for instance, records the lament of the common folk to the slaughter of their offspring: The commoners always suffered.

The reaction of the nobility of England was another matter, and this the chroniclers did record. One of the children Arthur had taken was under the protection of Lot of Lothian and Orkney, accorded the honor due Lot's sons. By the date of that child's birth, Lot knew that the child was not his: It had been conceived at Caerleon, and he either suspected or knew who the father was, which gave him real cause for anger. But he was willing to claim the son as his own rather than repudiate his wife. And the child's disappearance gave him excuse for rebellion against his old enemy, who had dishonored him.

He had abundant allies. Some, indeed, were even then readying a blow against the High King. Ryons of Norgales, "wroth out of mind," the chroniclers said, was massing a host along the northern marshes of Arthur's Welsh territories to avenge the deaths of the children. His brother Nero marched beside him.

Lot called nine other allies to the rebellion: the Duke of Candebenet; Brandegor of Strangore; Claryaunce of Northumberland; the King with a Hundred Knights, whose land no one could name; Idres of Cornwall; Anguisshe of Ireland; King Cardelmans; the King of Carados; the King of Scotland. The forces assembled and moved southwest toward the marshes, sending heralds ahead to Ryons' armies.

But instead of joining Ryons and Nero they halted within a day's march of the Norgales host. Chroniclers later said that Merlin had appeared and beguiled Lot with false prophecy, but none told what that prophecy was. After a day had passed, however, a messenger arrived, bloodied and exhausted; he slid from his horse and gave his report to Lot: Ryons and Nero had been slain by Arthur's armies and all their warriors killed.

"Alas," Lot replied. "Had we been together, no host under heaven would have been able to match us." Nevertheless, he sig-

Near the Welsh border, Arthur met the forces of Lot and his rebel allies. As in every battle he had fought before, the High King won the day.

Wrought in gilded metal by Merlin, the twelve rebel rulers of Britain stood in effigy, bearing tapers that perpetually burned. The figure above them was Arthur, baring his implacable sword.

naled his companions and, with his son Gawain riding as squire by his side, he led the armies of the north toward the field where Arthur waited.

On a great plain embraced by bare mountains, the armies met. At the dawn of that day, rain had fallen; now the field lay dull and brown under a weak winter sun, muddy with the blood of battle, overhung by wheeling ravens. Along the northern edge of the plain, under the double eagle of Orkney, stretched the long line of the rebel forces, their lances upright, their great horses shifting restlessly, held in iron check while the warriors waited. Far across the field, in similar array, the helmets of Arthur's chevaliers gleamed; in the center of the line, a beacon for his people, floated the gold-crowned standard of the High King.

The rebel banners dipped and rose. The lines of knights trembled and began to move. They advanced, lance points wavering above their heads, at a walk that quickened to a trot, a canter, then a full gallop. The ground trembled as hoofs drummed out the rhythm of the charge. Lances swung down to battle position. Then, amid the ululating battle cries of the men and the shrieks of the horses, the armies crashed together.

Lances by the hundreds were shattered. Men and horses tangled in a wilderness of broken bodies and flailing hoofs. In the confusion of battle, the heralds who recorded it could see only isolated images: of Caliburn flashing fire as Arthur laid about him; of the brothers Balin and Balan, knights of Arthur who the heralds said fought so fiercely that none could tell whether they had been sent as angels from heaven or as devils from hell. And the heralds spoke always of Lot, the cornered bear, ferocious and unflinching, rallying his men to the double eagle again and yet again. "Alas," said the chroniclers. "He could not endure, which was a great pity, that so worthy a knight as he should be overmatched."

The heralds saw his death. Arthur's fellow, Pellinore of the Isles, pushed his way to the fore of the warriors who were pressing Lot; he raised his broadsword and swung. The blade was deflected, but it sliced into the neck of Lot's horse. The beast's lifeblood poured forth in a scarlet fountain, and the horse sank to its knees and rolled onto the ground.

In a moment, Lot was on his feet, swordless, facing Pellinore. And Pellinore swung again in a great stroke, "through the helmet and head unto the brows," splitting the northern King's head.

When Lot fell, the shattered remnants of the Orkney faction fled, all except young Gawain, who stood over his father's corpse, guarding it in death and crying vengeance on the killer, Pellinore. The field was left to Arthur and the carrion eaters that waited in the winter sky.

The High King walked among the bodies of his enemies; each of the rebel chieftains lay on the field in his own blood. Arthur had the bodies taken up with honor and borne south with his armies to Camelot. There they were buried with all that was due them. The tomb of Lot was placed separate from the rest and carved more richly to honor his valor, for Lot had brought himself glory by the manner of his dying, and Arthur was always generous in victory.

Merlin fashioned a token of that victory. From brass and copper gilded with gold he wrought images of each of the twelve chieftains who had fought Arthur. He clustered them together as they had died together, and over their heads he placed an image of the High King with his drawn sword raised in triumph.

Each of the rebel rulers held a lighted taper in his hand; each taper burned steadily day and night. They would burn, said the Enchanter, until he himself was dead and gone and no longer watched over the reign of the High King.

III

❧ GUINEVERE ❧

The High King's bride was brought to him in the spring of the year that followed his victories; she was the prize of peace and the promise of fair weather after storm. Even the heavens smiled upon her, the storytellers said. On the day of her arrival, the sky was a cloudless blue. Sunshine burnished the golden stone of the walls of Camelot and sparkled on the broad river that curled around the castle's foot.

The river was the bride's highway, for she journeyed to Arthur by water, sailing as smoothly as a swan in a royal barge canopied in silk and ornamented with gold. Her oarsmen were liveried in white, and the gilded blades flashed as they swept the water.

Past the willows whitening in the breeze, the pale barge glided, past stands of aspen, past green river reeds, into the shadow of Camelot's walls. The oars lifted in unison then, as the barge slid onto the riverbank. There, the High King himself waited to welcome his Queen. The common people were clustered nearby, but they caught only a glimpse of her as she stepped from the barge and took the King's outstretched hands. They saw a tall young woman, her shining hair floating loose around her shoulders, as became a maiden; her underdress, called a cote-hardie, was as pale as moonlight, and the trailing panels of her overdress were edged in silver miniver. The courtiers of Camelot gathered around her, bright as birds of many colors, and hid her from view.

The maiden was Guinevere, daughter to Leodegran of Camelerd. She was the lily of the west, the storytellers said, the only maiden worthy of Arthur the King. Yet Merlin the Enchanter had disputed Arthur's choice: In a voice as bleak as the winter wind, Merlin had told the High King that Guinevere would bring him sorrow. Arthur, mighty in victory, ignored the old man's warnings, and Merlin was silenced.

Leodegran felt nothing but joy, and he expressed it handsomely. For Guinevere's dowry he gave a hundred knights to Arthur's service. He also sent to the High King an enormous table, constructed in Uther Pendragon's time; its shape, a perfect circle, reflected the perfection of the company of warriors that Arthur was forming. Among that company, besides the knights of Leodegran and knights who had fought beside

❧ ❧ ❧ ❧ ❧ ❧ ❧ ❧ ❧ ❧ ❧ ❧ ❧ ❧ ❧

A true warrior was young Gawain of Orkney, knighted on King Arthur's wedding day. His name, the poets said, meant "hawk of May."

Arthur, were three of the sons of Lot of Orkney. Arthur had kept them by him to train among his own people; their mother, Morgause, he had banished to her Orkney holdings. She had Lot's youngest son in her care. The eldest of the young men, Gawain, was knighted on Arthur's wedding day.

So the marriage was made and the days of feasting began. On the floor of the High King's hall, primroses and lavender were strewn among the rushes for sweetness. The long trestle tables gleamed with gold: with the nef, in the shape of a ship, used for holding the salt; with chased dishes divided to contain cloves, mace, saffron, cinnamon, cumin, aniseed and coriander, the spices that the courtiers loved; with ewers and basins for the bathing of hands; with the heavy platters that bore swans, peacocks, partridges and pheasants, all of them roasted, then re-dressed in their feathers; with bowls for the stews of venison, rabbit, boar and pork. The amount of food was kingly indeed: A meal might offer only three courses—announced by a fanfare of trumpets—but the courses consisted of thirty dishes each.

The feasting hall was full of sound and movement. Pages moved to and fro, bearing dishes. Among the rushes, the King's hounds played and fed on scraps that were thrown their way. Above the celebrants, hooded in velvet, their jesses ornamented by silver bells, the King's hawks shifted on their perches. Higher still, in an oriel, harpists played and minstrels sang.

Guinevere presided by the King's side, her brown hair now braided and coiled over her ears in the seemly scrolls of a wife and covered with a net of gold. She had the composure proper to a queen, with a glance of peculiar sweetness and a becoming modesty that showed in the swift rose that bloomed in her pale skin when she bent her head under her husband's smile. "She is passing welcome," Arthur had said when he greeted her at the river. "I have loved her long, and therefore nothing is so dear to me as she." And it was true, as all could see; the King's ease and delight illumined the feasting and brought pleasure to all the company.

❧ ❧ ❧ ❧ ❧ ❧ ❧ ❧ ❧ ❧ ❧ ❧ ❧ ❧ ❧

But Merlin's mood was different. Although he gave her the courtesy that was her due, his look was grave. The Queen made no comment on this, thinking, perhaps, that such was the Enchanter's habitual demeanor. But Kay, the seneschal, flushed with wine and bristling in his brother's defense, said at last in his surly, stuttering way, "These long looks poorly suit the wedding feast, old man."

Merlin replied: "Guinevere brings Arthur's sorrow, and she is here by his choice."

"It seems not. She brings him joy. Perhaps your magic has left you." Kay took a drink of wine and opened his mouth to make further observations; he shut it again, however, when he caught the Enchanter's cold gaze.

"You were ever an ill speaker, Kay," said Merlin. "You would do well to remember that my powers will not leave unless I let them go."

"Show your powers then," said Kay. Heads turned, for the seneschal had spoken loudly. A little silence fell in the great chamber.

"My skills are not for idle show. To use them at all—especially to use them lightly—invites attention from the old ones, who become vigilant when magic ruffles the air. Their eyes will turn toward us. And their gaze we will be safer without." Kay made the sign that averted evil, and around him, several older knights did the same.

Then the Queen smiled, breaking the tension. She said, "Lord Enchanter, we do not ask as a challenge to your power. Only make me an illusion for my bride gift, to give me pleasure."

And after a moment had passed, Merlin nodded. "Madam, as you wish," he said. "If you will come to me in your own tower court when the sun stands at noon, I will make an enchantment for you."

Almost as elusive as the folk of Faerie, Guinevere bore a name to match her character. The word was Welsh for "white phantom."

On a hill by a river Camelot rose, strong-walled, silvery-towered. This was the chief fortress of Arthur and the measure of his might: No human foe could breach its high walls.

His dark robes billowing out around him, the old man turned and left the hall.

An hour later—for feasts in those days began at ten in the morning—the courtiers walked, in twos and threes, to the courtyard that lay before the building called the Queen's Tower, a pretty, sunny place, bordered by flowering pear and apple trees, that Arthur had built for his bride's pleasure. The Enchanter awaited them; his cloak was thrown back to reveal that he wore a sword. At his feet lay a small linen sack. A curious expression—a mountebank's leer—twisted his austere features.

The courtiers formed a whispering ring around him. Guinevere, her eyes as bright as a child's, signaled for the enchantment to begin.

"I give you old magic that I learned in Wales. This feat is not my own," Merlin said. With a glance at Kay the doubter, he added, "I summon the clouds." Lightly and slowly, tendrils and puffs of white drifted down from the blue and curled the tower roof, spreading to form a snowy ceiling forty feet above the Enchanter's head. Cool shadow fell on the tiles of the courtyard.

"And a ladder to the sky." From the linen sack, the Enchanter drew a coil of rope, which he held flat across both outstretched hands. He began to whistle, a reedy, wailing melody. In response, the rope trembled. Unwinding itself coil by coil, swaying serpent-like to the tune of Merlin's song, the rope ascended until one end vanished into the whiteness of the cloud and its long length hung straight, dangling free above the paving tiles.

"And a hare for the hunt." The Enchanter reached into the sack once more and withdrew from it a tiny creature, no bigger than a mouse. He held it to his lips and whispered over it, and as he whispered, the creature swelled until it took the form of a living hare, pale gray of fur and black of eye. Its ears twitched enquiringly as Merlin spoke. Then the Enchanter lifted his hand swiftly, as if sending a bird into flight, and the hare swarmed up the rope like a cat, disappearing into the cloud.

"And a maiden to hunt the hare." The sack yielded a little doll in the shape of a peasant girl. Merlin set it on the pavement and whispered once again, and before the company's eyes, the doll grew and trembled into life. A maiden stood among them, blinking uncertainly and glancing from face to face. At her master's command, however, she grasped the rope and climbed it hand over hand until she touched the cloud. She reached for it as if it were solid earth and pulled herself up until she, too, disappeared into whiteness. The last that was seen of her was her bare dangling feet.

Observing his audience solemnly staring upward, caught in his spell, Merlin added with a wink, "And a man to comfort the maid," and dug into the linen sack once more. This time his catch grew into a sturdy, comely youth who grinned at his creator and swiftly climbed the rope into the cloud country above. The courtiers relaxed into laughter: This was a lusty conceit, suitable for a wedding feast. Even Kay laughed at the commotion above their heads, as the maiden in the cloud squealed and gasped and then fell silent, save for muffled giggles.

But Merlin's face took on a tight-lipped, sour look. "This is not comfort, but mischief," he said. He snapped his fingers once. The giggles from the maiden ceased, and a moment later, the young woman he had fashioned slipped from the cloud and landed panting at his feet. Her tumbled hair and unlaced bodice told the tale of her adventure, and she hid her face from the courtiers' smiles.

Once more Merlin snapped his summons. In answer, the youth appeared, dropping lightly to the pavement with the hare in his arms. He gave a bow to the company and one to Merlin; then he reached for the maiden. But Merlin said, "For shame, for shame, to seduce a young maiden. Let her be." He turned to Kay, the seneschal: "Surely the seducer deserves to pay a penalty?"

"Aye," Kay said, grinning. "He has vigor but lacks virtue."

In the next moment, the grin froze on his face. With a sudden movement, the Enchanter drew his sword and swung it. The young man's head fell to the ground. For an instant his body stayed upright, a fountain of blood throbbing into the air and spattering the pavement and the ladies' robes. Then the body, too, fell.

Arthur thrust his white-faced Queen behind him and said, "This

Merlin made magic for an amusement —
a hare that climbed like a cat. The exercise was
dangerous: It drew the eyes of Faerie.

With days of feasting, with music and singing, with all the ceremony of the royal court, Arthur took Guinevere

elerd to wife. A huntress of the other world broke in upon the festivity, pursuing an enchanted stag as white as snow.

is madness. Death is too severe a punishment for a dalliance you yourself invented, Merlin. What bride gift is this that you have made?"

"You find me too severe?" the Enchanter replied. "Well then, I must needs make a happy ending." He stooped over the body and the head so that his robes hid both from view. Then he stood back, and the young man arose, alive once more by Merlin's magic.

But something was awry. The youth stared at them, mouthing silently. His features faced over his shoulder blades, and his feet shuffled in his own blood. His head had been put on backward.

"Oh, pity of God," said Kay. "It is better that he die than live like that."

"No punishment at all, then?" said Merlin. With one hand, he twisted the young man's head until it faced forward again. Then he touched man, maiden and hare in turn; they shrank to the size of toys, and he thrust them into the sack. A whistle brought the rope, and it coiled itself away. Above the courtiers' heads, the cloud faded into ribbons and blew away.

"You do ill to doubt my powers, Kay," said Merlin, adding to the Queen, "See, lady, it was illusion. Even the blood has gone." Then he, too, vanished.

So ended the entertainment, as capricious in its mixture of delight and horror, of promise and threat, as the Enchanter himself. But that exercise of magic, trivial in itself, did seem to stir the air and arouse the attention of the folk of Faerie, as Merlin had said it would. It was as if in playing with the power that he shared with the old ones by virtue of his fairy blood, the Enchanter opened wide a door to them, making the human men and women he counseled—and himself as well— vulnerable to their weapons.

The first of the old ones' incursions came almost at once, in the form of a drama played out in the High King's own hall. Arthur's wedding feast continued, as great feasts did then, through many days. And on a morning two days after the incident in the Queen's courtyard, the feasting was disrupted. Into the hall—unseen, it turned out, by the guards outside—a white stag leaped, its flanks streaked with a gray foam of sweat and blood showing at its nostrils. It tore through the chamber, pursued by a brachet—a dog that hunted by scent. Behind the brachet, a pack of coursing hounds streamed, and in their midst was a woman astride a white horse. She was a pale creature, crowned by the darkness of her flying hair; she wore the green gown of Faerie, and around her neck was slung an ivory hunting horn.

So wild was the gallop of prey and huntress, so sudden their advent and un- earthly their cries, that the men and the women in the hall were struck still in their places. But the scene was over in a matter of seconds. The animals careered around the tables; from out of the air, a warrior appeared and seized the brachet; another man captured the huntress, and these vanished from the hall. The stag and the hounds escaped the chamber, leaving behind a trail of overturned tables and benches, of

❧ ❧ ❧ ❧ ❧ ❧ ❧ ❧ ❧ ❧ ❧ ❧ ❧ ❧ ❧ ❧ ❧

broken glass and crumpled gold.

In an instant, the High King was on his feet, but before he could issue orders, Merlin forestalled him. The Enchanter sent three knights out: one to follow the stag and bring back its head, one to find the brachet and one to free the huntress. These knights obeyed him; they rode into the realm of Faerie, the chroniclers said, and found what they sought, returning weeks later with the stag's head and the brachet and word that the huntress was safe in her own lands. But the knights' adventures are not important to the story. What mattered was the meaning of the invasion of the hall — a meaning that was plain only to Merlin. After commanding the three knights to take up the pursuit, he stood gray-faced beside the King. His cheeks were sunken, as if he were a corpse; his eyes had the dull stare of the dead; his hands trembled.

"What ails you, Lord Enchanter?" cried the Queen.

When he answered, his voice was an old man's, cracked and weak. "She has come then," he said. "Still young, still un-

Queen Guinevere rode out on the first day of May to gather white hawthorn as a guard against the fairies. It proved an ill-judged mission: Forces of the other world awaited her.

schooled. And she has come through my own fault; I opened the gate that let her in."

"Who is the huntress?" asked the High King.

"Niniane is her name."

He would say no more, except that he was done with prophecy. That night, he left the fortress, and he did not return.

Before the month was out, the forces of the old ones struck again. May Eve, then called Beltane Eve, arrived. It was a sacred time, the hours that divided winter from

*Melwas of the Summer Country, concealed by a cloak of invisibility, snatched
Queen Guinevere and took her away to his own lands. His fortress was hidden from human view, but
Arthur had more than once bested an otherworldly enemy, and he would do so again.*

summer, and throughout the High King's realm, the people made festival to drive away the fairies, who were free to roam that night, and to welcome in the season of growth and fecundity.

At moonrise on that night, bonfires were kindled, each with nine branches gathered from nine different trees by nine men. On every hill these fires blazed, miniature suns honoring the life-giving sun of heaven. And all around the fires, the people played out their ancient rituals, asking for health and growth. They baked Beltane cakes of barley and oats, round as the sun. These cakes were broken up and divided by lot, some pieces being designated as offerings for wolves, so that the predators might spare the lambs, and some for crows, so that the hungry birds might spare the chicks. One piece in each cake was blackened by charcoal, and the unlucky person who drew it became the Beltane carline, the sacrificial victim offered against the dangers that threatened human health. The carline's neighbors made a mime of casting him into their Beltane fire; throughout that year he would be called a dead man. The farmers drove their cattle through the fires, too, to protect the animals from disease. And all night long, the people's pipes and little drums sounded across the fields, calling the measure from the hillsides while men and women danced sunwise around the flames, black silhouettes against the gold, welcoming the season of light.

Just before dawn, when the fires were dwindling and the dancers trailing down from the hills, the women who had not danced left their halls and cottages and went into the countryside to see the summer sunrise and to bring in the May. They cut branches of hawthorn, the fairies' flower. These branches they wove into wreaths to give them greater efficacy, and with the wreaths they garlanded every door, to protect each household from the folk of Faerie.

Among the women was Guinevere, the very Queen of the May, people said, for in her marriage to the High King she had become—like the May queens crowned with flowers in every British village—the mother of the fields' fertility. Adorned in her bridal white and gold, she rode out of Camelot on a white horse caparisoned with gilded bells; her pages walked beside her and her squires and ladies rode behind. None of them carried sterner weapons than hunting knives, but all the weapons of the kingdom would have availed them nothing against the beings that walked abroad in those dawn hours.

Guinevere did not come back to her husband's hall that day. The pages and squires who had been her escort returned to Camelot without her. Rigid with terror, they stood before the High King and swore that they had seen nothing more than a mist or a cloud or a white radiance, a veil of light that enfolded the Queen and then vanished into the air, leaving her horse riderless. They could not defend her, they stammered: The attack had come and gone more quickly than a man could draw a single breath.

Arthur had them thrown in prison. Then he set out to search for the Queen.

To show his skill in the ways of magic, Merlin built a castle in the air, a bagatelle for the fairy Niniane.

She asked for the secrets of Merlin's power; when she had them, she danced spells to enchant the Enchanter.

When he awoke from Niniane's spell, Merlin found himself a prisoner in the aerial palace he had fashioned.

Through every corner of the land his riders went; through every village rode small bands of knights, grim of face and cold of voice. The word spread among the people: Without the Queen's presence, the crops would fail and the land would die. And after some months, whispers reached the ears of the riders. The Queen lay at Glastonbury, a prisoner of Melwas, the Summer Country King, who if he was not himself an old one, had fairy protection. No one could tell for certain: Melwas' fortress—reputed to be built of glass—lay hidden within the hill called Glastonbury Tor. And the Tor rose in the midst of a vast waterland. The position was invulnerable, wrote the chroniclers, "due to the fortifications of thicket, reed and marsh."

But Arthur's power was matchless then. The accounts of his actions are incomplete—and some are contradictory. The clearest version of the affair was left by monks who had settled in a small abbey at Glastonbury itself. According to them, Arthur raised an enormous army from kingdoms in Devon and Cornwall; with this army, he threatened to lay waste the Summer Country and open the Tor itself. At that point, the Glastonbury abbot and a monk called Gildas persuaded Melwas to release the Queen unharmed; it was they who arranged the truce that saved the land. So the threat of his own might—and the elders of the church—defeated the first strike at Arthur's heart. He had Guinevere safe again at his side.

But where was Merlin the Enchanter, he who should have brought his magic to defend the King against the forces of the other world? He had not been seen since the night he left Camelot. Only slowly, over months and years, did his story filter back, in minstrels' songs, in fragments of verse, in cryptic utterances from the old ones. He had gone to an island in the sea, said some; he was trapped within a tree by magic. But some chronicles told another tale:

Merlin left Arthur in order to follow his own fate, which he had discerned in the High King's feasting hall. His lot, it seemed, was to be reduced to a fool, an object of pity among those who had honored him. Sick with a desire induced by enchantment, he journeyed through England and across the sea to Brittany, pursuing the huntress Niniane, a daughter of Faerie, as he had known at once.

No humiliation was spared him, no silly behavior of a fond old man. He could travel as a deer for swiftness, as a hare or an owl for secrecy, but he made this journey in the guise of a young and handsome squire, hiding by illusion his white hair and raddled face—in the pathetic hope that his looks would please Niniane.

Because he was led by magic, he found her soon enough, in the forest of Brocé-liande, a haunted place still within the rule of the other world. Decked in his false finery, he strode along a track that opened among the trees, and if he felt the eyes that watched him or heard the cruel laughter that rustled the leaves and crackled the branches, he gave no sign. The track led him to a clearing on the crest of a hill. There on the grass sat the fairy huntress, pale and lovely and remote as a star, regarding him with eyes so wide and soft that the mortal in him trembled for her, even while the half that was not mortal withdrew in fear. He took her hand, as any gallant might, and offered her his heart. Niniane drew her hand away and shook her head. She needed no young squire, she said.

"I am more than a squire," the Enchanter replied. "See what my skill can make for you." He turned her so that she looked into the sky, and in the clouds he made her a palace. Stone by enchanted stone he built it, high above the birds' paths, adding for her pleasure soaring towers with roofs of gold, silken pennants that fluttered in the breeze, trees and flowers that grew where no land was. The whole splendid creation floated high above the forest, serene in the empyrean.

As he made this illusion, the trappings of false youth slipped from him, but the fairy seemed not to notice; indeed, it would be surprising if she had not known him for what he was in any case.

"This is a wonder," she told him. "You are the master of enchantments my people have lost. Will you not teach them to me?" She smiled upon him, a secret smile filled with sweet promise. And Merlin gave the fairy what she asked. Hour after hour, he sat beside her. Singing the melodies that

*In the clouds, held by fairy magic, the Enchanter lived,
lost forever to the King he had served.*

made his magic, chanting the runes that shaped his spells, he gave Niniane his power. Illusion he taught her, and knowledge of the future, the words that brought invisibility and the thoughts that changed shape. With his old hands, he sketched the gestures that brought weapons from the air and forged chains no man could break; he gave her the secrets of battle and of entrapment.

For days they stayed together in the green forest clearing while Niniane listened and smiled her secret smile and stroked the Enchanter's hand. And at last one after-noon, when the sunlight lay warm and still on his white hair, Merlin's voice faded into silence. In his long speaking, he had emptied himself of might, and now he lay on the grass, no more for the moment than an old man, frail as any old man is frail, left with nothing more than the memory of glory.

Then, with infinite gentleness, Niniane laid her hand upon his hair and said, "I have learned what you teach. Now I will give you rest, as you have taught me to do." In the softest of voices she began to sing to him. She rose and danced as she sang, and as she danced, she drew from her waist the floating girdle of silk that bound her robe. She dropped one end of the girdle at Merlin's feet. Tears glistened in his eyes as he watched her; then the heavy lids drooped, and Merlin slept.

hen he awoke, he lay on a pallet on a stone floor, surrounded by curving walls of stone. Niniane stood beside him, coiling her girdle in her hands. Her song had stopped; the glance she gave him was cool and calm. "Do not believe that I will leave you here alone, Merlin," she said. "I will be here with you, from time to time." Then she turned and walked through a narrow door.

The old Enchanter slowly rose and followed where she had gone. At the door, he halted, staring dully out. Above his head, the gilded turrets of a palace soared. At his feet, all around the steps that led from the door, clouds puffed and curled and shifted, sometimes opening as a veil opens, to reveal the hills and treetops of Brocéliande, far, far below.

Ever living, ever estranged from the world of men and women, from the scenes of his power and the halls of the High King, Merlin was trapped in the prison that he himself had built. The masters of the other world, using Niniane, had taken him away from Arthur the King.

IV

✣ MORGAN ✣

hree Queens were sisters to Arthur, three women linked by blood and, it seems, by service to the old ones. The eldest, Morgause, brought a shadow early to Arthur's life. She had tempted him; she had lain with him; she had borne him the son who was prophesied to be a sword against him. Then, having done the deed, she retreated into exile on her cold Orkney island, rearing the child in secret, nourishing him until his time to act should come. Of the middle sister – Elaine of Garlot – the chroniclers had little to say, save that she remained in her own lands, remote from the High King and apparently harmless to him. The youngest sister, however, kept close to the High King for many years, an ever-present enemy, although she concealed her nature as long as she could. She was the Queen of Gorre, and she was the most powerful of the triad.

This sister's given name was Morgan, and she was also called le Fay – or fairy – because of the magic that was in her. It was said that she had a home in the other world, that her youth had been spent secluded in an island convent of the old ones, learning the secret ways of enchantment. According to some accounts, she had served on the Isle of Glass as one of the nine guardians of the caldron of inspiration that Arthur seized in his youth. Some said she had been schooled by Merlin; some claimed that she was Niniane, in different guise. Morgan understood the stars, people came to believe, and all the ways of healing; she could fly in raven form and hide herself in a spider's shape. Every subtle art was hers.

But this was not apparent during Morgan's first years at Camelot. She was one among many who became part of the High King's court, as the sun of his power climbed toward its apogee. With her husband Urien, she occupied chambers in the fortress. Just as Urien served among Arthur's warriors and her son Yvain trained among his squires, Morgan joined the company of the Queen's ladies-in-waiting. She was a handsome woman, but she was much given to solitude; she kept herself apart from Guinevere's other ladies and, it seems, from the knights who flocked around the Queen, a little court of blameless admirers. She was an oddity in a company so close as Arthur's then was, and this – with the singing that floated from her chambers in the

✣ ✣ ✣ ✣ ✣ ✣ ✣ ✣ ✣ ✣ ✣ ✣ ✣ ✣ ✣

night, with the ravens that came at her call and fed from her hand, as if they were doves – caused talk. Although she did not presume on her kinship to the High King, it protected her from more severe comment – that and the presence of her husband and her son, men so valiant and so loyal that none dared speak a word against her.

In fact, Morgan was loose with the younger knights of Arthur's court. She had the certain age and knowingness that attracted them, and she drew power from their desire. At first, she concealed her activities, but as time went on, she grew careless – or perhaps too arrogant to bother with discretion. She gathered her own circle of gallants, and it became apparent from the quarrels that developed among them, and from Urien's long looks, that the knights' affection for her was far from blameless. Where Morgan moved, quiet and smiling, clouds of ill will seemed to gather and factions to form.

One spring afternoon, Guinevere entered a sunny chamber to find Morgan and a knight named Guiomar – Guinevere's own cousin – hidden in a deep window embrasure. Their whispering, quickly halted, and Guiomar's guilty glance showed clearly enough how the land lay. The Queen surveyed them; she was a new bride, and honor and loyalty had been bred into her soul. After some moments, she said to Guiomar, "You have my leave to go. I will take this matter to the High King." To Morgan she added, "You were best with your lord Urien, lady." Morgan's response was a bland smile. She curtsied and slipped past the Queen and out of the room.

The result of the discovery was that Guiomar was sent from court, to cool his hot blood in Arthur's northern garrisons. He left without protest and without bidding Morgan farewell; the liaison with the Queen of Gorre had been dark and tiring, and he was glad to be free of it, to be riding in the clear air, away from the shadowed, overscented chambers where Morgan's enchantment had held him. Morgan stayed, for Arthur would not allow her husband to be shamed. Her public conduct was more seemly after that, for a while.

But she was merely biding her time until opportunity arose to avenge the humiliation. In secret, she turned to another paramour, a man named Accolon of Gaul. In secret, she fashioned weapons of magic to wield against the High King. And one summer afternoon, she used them.

Arthur hunted all that day in the hills beyond Camelot. Late in the afternoon, following a great deer, he left his comrades and plunged into a stand of trees. Deep into the tangles of the wood he rode. Behind him, the hunters' voices faded, until the only sounds were the crackling of the underbrush and his horse's heavy breathing.

The wood gave way at last to a meadow that sloped down to a riverbank. On the bank lay the deer. It was dead. But the animal drew no more than a glance from the High King, for beyond it, rocking gently in the river current, was a crystal boat with sails of membranous silk; the little craft was so pale and insubstantial that it appeared to be compounded of the water and the river mist. Although no hand guided it, the boat turned and slid onto the sandy bank as Arthur approached.

This was a vessel of Faerie, a challenge from the old ones and an invitation to adventure. As any knight who prized his valor would have, Arthur took the dare: He dismounted, gave his horse a slap on the flank to send it home and stepped aboard. At once, the boat slipped into the water and moved downriver, its silken sails swelling with a wind from the other world. Through the waning afternoon, the fairy boat sailed, following the river as it twisted and turned into an unknown country, hidden behind a wall of heavy trees that swayed and sighed and whispered on the bank. At last the day faded; yet light danced along the gunwales of the boat, sparkling on the crystal. In that candleglow of enchantment, Arthur slept.

He awakened to darkness and cold, to prison stench, to the dull clinking of iron shackles and the

In a convent on an enchanted isle, Arthur's half-sister Morgan learned the arts of illusion, spirit-summoning and the shifting of shape.

muffled mutterings of imprisoned men. He spoke, and he was answered. His fellow prisoners were British knights, captured by a lord called Damas to serve in a battle against his brother over their inheritance. When each knight refused — as each did, for Damas was a cruel and petty tyrant and his brother a good man — he was thrown into prison. Some of them had been in the pit for years. Arthur listened in silence, waiting for word from Damas' messenger.

It came within the hour. A heavy door swung open; the figure of a woman stood in the arch, outlined by the flame of the torch she carried. Blinking in the brightness, Arthur said, "Lady, are you not a member of the High King's court?" But the woman shook her head; she was the daughter of Damas, she said, and a stranger to the court. She would not look at him, but she gave him her father's message: If he would stand as Damas' champion, he would go free.

"If these knights-prisoner are freed before the battle, I will fight for Damas," the

Consort to Urien of Gorre, Morgan served with her husband at Arthur's court. But Morgan was no true wife, as Guinevere discovered. She seduced the Queen's own cousin; the young man was sent from Camelot.

High King replied. And that was done. The knights were freed from their shackles; guards led them away. Arthur also was freed, to await the return of Damas' daughter. When she appeared, she brought a shield and armor – and his own sword, Caliburn, in its jeweled scabbard. With these, she herself armed him.

"Lady, how came you by my sword?" said Arthur, staring down at her. But her face was hidden by a curtain of dark hair. She whispered, "It was sent to me by the Queen, your sister Morgan le Fay." She would say no more.

The maiden led him to a high hall where torches flared upon the wall, and in the flickering light, he saw the man he was to battle: a tall man, his face hidden in shadow, who stood leaning easily on a sword as fine, it seemed, as his own. The maiden withdrew out of range to watch. Without a word, Arthur swung his shield across his body and drew his own sword in the salute. The weapon was strangely heavy and lifeless in his hand.

Nevertheless, he raised it high, and before his opponent could parry, he struck. Arthur's blade glanced harmlessly off the other man's shield, and as he completed the swing, the warrior's sword flashed fire in the air, cutting in under Arthur's guard and sliding through his mailed sleeve into his arm. Hot blood soaked through the mail as he returned the thrust. Had Caliburn been in his hand, his strikes would have been lethal; had its scabbard hung at his side, no blade could have cut him. He was, it seemed, without its protection.

Yet Arthur fought on regardless. Grunting with effort, the two men swung and thrust, and Arthur took cut after cut, until he trembled with weakness and pain. Finding his own blade almost useless, he wielded the sword as a club, bringing it down again and again on his enemy's helmet, sending the man staggering dizzily back. Two hours passed while the fiery sword flashed in the air and Arthur bled. Still he fought on, unflinching. His enemy beat him to his knees. Arthur thrust upward, under the man's shield, and his own sword snapped at the hilt. The man raised his weapon for a final, deadly stroke. But the great sword flew flaming from his hand, an arc of light in the air, and clattered to the floor. The warrior swayed a little where he stood, rubbing his hand. His head swung uncertainly from side to side, seeking the cause of the sword's leap.

The cause was a tall woman who had appeared in the hall – a woman of Faerie, from her pale look. In a high voice as chill as the waters of a mountain lake, she cried, "That sword is Caliburn. It belongs to the water folk, but it is in the High King's keeping while he lives. You have no right to bear it, knight." Then she was gone, even before the echo of her words against the stones ceased.

Arthur caught up the sword. "You have been away from me all too long, and much damage have you done me," he cried to it. In the same breath, he shouted at his adversary, "Much pain have you given me with this sword. Now it offers your death."

He ripped Caliburn's healing scabbard from the man's side and sent it spinning across the stones of the floor. Then he brought Caliburn down in a mighty swing that tore into the side of the stranger's helmet. The man fell, blood bubbling from mouth and nose and ears, and in an instant Arthur was kneeling beside him, tearing his helmet from his head in order to deal the death blow. The helmet slid off, revealing the man's white, agonized face. It was Accolon of Gaul.

Voices murmured at the door; the dark maiden had disappeared, but the lord of the castle, Damas, and his brother crowded into the room with their people and heard the words of Accolon: "Woe that I had the sword, for it has made my death."

how came you by the sword? How came you to fight your own lord?" the High King demanded. And Accolon then told how, by her arts, his lover Morgan had made a counterfeit of Caliburn the Dauntless; how she had given the counterfeit to the King and stolen his own sword for Accolon; how she plotted against the King's life and sought also to take the life of her husband, Urien, so that she and Accolon might seize the throne by force and give the land into the hands of the old ones.

Having spoken, Accolon turned his head aside and died. Arthur's own hand closed the knight's eyes. Then he said to the watching group, "Which of you is Damas?"

"Lord, I am he." A man stepped forward, offering his sword hilt in submission.

The High King said, "You were a pawn in this matter, Damas. It was little you knew that you had the High King to fight your battles. For that I excuse you and leave you with your life. For your other deeds, I make this judgment: Your lands shall go to your brother and you shall serve as his vassal. And you shall ride upon a lady's palfrey until you prove yourself worthy of the destrier of a knight." He paused and wiped the blood from his eyes. Then he said, "Accolon was a man of more courage than judgment. Lay his body on a horse bier and carry it to my fortress at Camelot. Convey it to my sister of Gorre, and say that I send it as a present to her. Tell her that I have Caliburn and the scabbard. Say further that when I am healed of my wounds, I will deal with her." He swayed where he stood then, but the servants of Damas were there to catch him before he fell. They carried him to a manor on Damas' lands, where women lived who understood the arts of healing, and there he lay for some weeks.

As for Morgan, said the chroniclers, she proceeded with her plan. They recorded that on the night of Arthur's battle she had crept to Urien's bedside, armed with a sword to murder her husband. She stood for some moments by the bed, gazing down at him with grim satisfaction — and that pause saved Urien's life. Morgan's son, warned by a waiting woman, appeared and wrenched the sword away. He might have killed her then, but Morgan was too shrewd for such a young man as he. She fell weeping to her knees, claiming that a demon had enchanted her and that now she was free again, and her son believed these words.

Arthur knew nothing of these events. The place where he lay was remote and quiet.

❧ ❧ ❧ ❧ ❧ ❧ ❧ ❧ ❧ ❧ ❧ ❧ ❧ ❧ ❧

The women who served there did not speak; instead, they communicated with one another by signs. Their heavy black robes made only the faintest sighs as they trailed along the floor. In that peaceful chamber, Caliburn remained always in Arthur's grip, its scabbard on the floor by the bed.

One night, however, the peace was broken. The clink of metal roused the King from his sleep. Grasping the sword tightly, he turned his head and in the feeble rushlight saw Caliburn's scabbard clutched in a woman's hand. Jewels glinted and a skirt rustled. An instant later, hoofs clattered on the cobblestones outside. At once, Arthur was on his feet, shouting orders to the women who cared for him. They armed him as he commanded; they saddled him a horse; and they showed the direction that the dark woman and her men had taken. They cringed before his anger, but they were helpless. The woman had been crowned; she had given orders that the High King not be awakened to greet her, and they had done as they were bidden.

He spurred his horse and galloped out of the abbey court and into the forest beyond. Through the small hours he rode, with no more than moonlight to show him the path. At last, when the dawn came and a mist lay on the ground and clung to the trunks of the trees, he heard hoofbeats and low calls ahead. The trees gave way to plain. A lake was there, sullen in the dull light. The jewels of Caliburn's scabbard gleamed for an instant above the water. Then the scabbard vanished, and widening rings rippled outward.

On the shore, stone statues stood. The King moved among them and observed them with thoughtful eyes. By the water, Morgan rode, frozen into rock; all around her stood her men, caught fast in the attitudes they had taken when struck. So lifelike were the figures, so seemingly filled with action, that he rode close and touched them. But they were no

Ever active, Morgan sought to murder Urien and free herself for the sake of a lover. It was her son Yvain who stayed her hand and saved his father's life.

A crystal ship of Faerie beckoned the High King to adventure. After he stepped aboard it, the

him down a winding river, through a country he did not know and into a place of darkness.

The crystal ship carried Arthur into battle with Morgan's paramour, Accolon, who wielded Arthur's own mighty sword.

...gh King would have died then, but for the sword's fairy guardian. She sent Caliburn flying from the false knight's hand.

Arthur defeated Accolon, but Morgan captured the healing scabbard of the sword Caliburn. The King pursued

the enchantress eluded him: She cast the scabbard into a lake, then turned herself and her companions to stone.

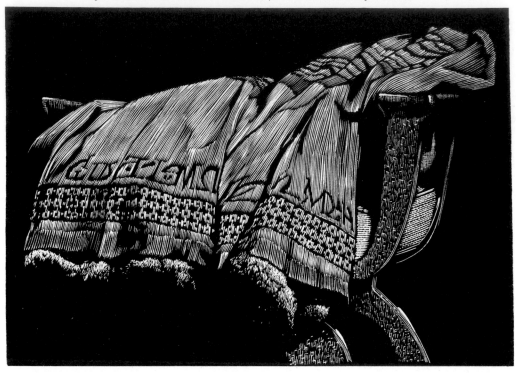

more than stones, cold and dank already from the mist. The place was silent.

"A fitting punishment for the witch and her people," Arthur said. Then he wheeled the horse about and headed home.

Urien awaited him there, bleak-faced and gray for the dishonor done his name by his wife. He offered his life to erase the stain, but Arthur would not have it. He offered to depart for his own lands, but the High King refused to send him into exile. Urien was a loyal man and a strong ally. Yvain his son was another matter: The youth appeared too much a dupe of his mother. Arthur discharged him from court for a year, to prove his valor by adventure. Hotheaded Gawain of Orkney, incensed at the insult to his cousin, left with him. So even in death, it seemed, Morgan caused dissension.

But Morgan was not dead, nor was she bound in enchantment. Messengers began to arrive from her. The first was a young man named Manassen, a roughhewn knight who spoke in the rolling tones of those who lived by the western sea. He rode into Camelot unescorted and surrendered his weapons to the High King's men-at-arms, announcing that he had come as a herald for a lady and that his life was protected by the service he performed. It was true — and fortunate for Manassen: When he delivered his message in the High King's hall, Arthur's face grew white with rage.

"I come from the lady Morgan le Fay," said Manassen. "She bids me tell you that she does not fear you while she has the power to turn herself and her servants to stone and bring them back to life again. She says that she will stay now in her lands of Gorre and that the castles and towns in her rule are proof against any army. She says that at the end of your life, it is she who will welcome you into the world of the dead."

"A kind sister," was Arthur's answer. "Give this man food and drink and send him on his way."

After that, there was silence from the enchantress. The summer deepened into autumn, and the fortress of Camelot drew in upon itself. From the fields around the castle, the wheat, barley and rye were brought in and stored in tall barns. The apples were gathered and piled in drying sheds. In November, called "the bloody month," those animals that could not be fed through the winter were driven to the fortress—the cattle from the pastures, the pigs from the forests where they had run half-wild, fattening on chestnuts and acorns. Then they were slaughtered and the meat salted down for the lean season. From different parts of Britain, those of Arthur's warriors who had ridden out to find adventure returned, battered and weary, to the protection of Camelot: Summer, not winter, was the fighting season. On winter nights in the King's smoky hall, these venturers told their tales to please Arthur and his Queen.

And on one winter afternoon, when the snow lay thick on roof and field and the howling of wolves sounded in the forests, just before the curfew was blown to signify the closing of the castle gates, Camelot received Morgan's second messenger, a young woman who arrived on horseback, accompanied only by a page. She was a comely maiden, frail-seeming and so shy that her voice scarcely rose above a whisper.

The sentries sent the horses to the stables and the page to the kitchens. The maiden asked to speak to Guinevere. They took her to Kay the seneschal, who, seeing that she was harmless, led her through snowy lanes and courtyards to the Queen's Tower. Up a winding stair he took her, into a small chamber whose vaulted ceiling was fretted with stars. On the stone walls, brightly dressed huntsmen followed a deer that never was caught through green fields thick with a thousand flowers. In those painted fields, small animals—hare and fox, badger and hedgehog—forever played. Above them, wren and robin forever tumbled in the sky, silently caroling for the Queen. Her high bed, hung with tapestry, stood in this chamber; deerskin covered the stones of the floor, and a fire blazed in the deep hearth. Beside this fire, fur-cloaked against the cold, sat the Queen, who greeted the maiden kindly and asked for her message.

hen she saw what the young woman had brought and heard the tale she had to tell, Guinevere sent a young page to fetch the High King. Arthur appeared soon enough, shaking the snow from his hair and shoulders, and throwing his cloak back as he entered the chamber. The Queen pushed the maiden gently forward, signaling her to speak.

"My lady of Gorre, your sister, sends greetings, lord," the young woman said. "She desires that you take this gift from her, and she promises that in whatever way she has offended you, she will make amends, in what fashion you demand."

❧ ❧ ❧ ❧ ❧ ❧ ❧ ❧ ❧ ❧ ❧ ❧ ❧ ❧ ❧

At Arthur's command, Morgan's messenger slipped the cloak around her shoulders – and died,
as the High King would have died, in a blast of magic-made flame.

"Does she so?" said the High King. "Let us see the gift of peace."

It lay across the Queen's hearth stool, a cloak of creamy wool, into whose border a pattern of silver and gold had been woven; it was a beautiful guard against the winter, fit indeed for a king. The maiden said softly that Morgan herself had woven it. She lifted it from the stool and held it for Arthur to see.

A silvery echo slid along the walls of the room, no more than the memory of a voice, too faint for anyone to hear the words. Anyone, that is, except the High King. Arthur halted in the very act of reaching for the cloak. "Maiden," he said. "This cloak you have brought I wish first to see upon your shoulders."

Morgan's messenger stared up at the High King, and the rosy flush left by the winter chill faded from her cheeks. The maiden shook her head and backed slowly away from him, wordless for a moment. Then she whispered, "Lord, it is not seemly that I wear a king's garment."

"Nevertheless, you will wear it now," said Arthur. His voice was level, and the maid bowed her head, having no choice but to obey the command. With the slowest of movements, she shook out the fabric of the cloak, raised it and swung it around her back. It settled on her small shoulders and fell to the floor in sculptured folds.

She gave one cry only, a cry lost under the explosion of light and sound that followed. Up above her head the maiden's hair rose, each strand a crackling torch flame. Beneath it, her face blackened and peeled, the melting eyes staring blindly, the mouth stretched wide in a soundless scream. Guinevere covered her face from the sight, but the High King stood rigid, watching the cloak's fire devour the messenger sent by his sister. The maiden bent in an arch of agony; she fell in a whirlwind of flame. In the end, nothing but cinders and stain was left to show where she had stood.

"It is finished," said the High King to his wife. "We do well to remember that my sister moves in hiding, a dark creature given to the dark." He sent soldiers to find the maiden's page, but the child had vanished into the air, taken back perhaps by Morgan's enchantments to the fortress where she laired.

❦ ❦ ❦ ❦ ❦ ❦ ❦ ❦ ❦ ❦ ❦ ❦ ❦ ❦ ❦ ❦

The Lady turned to her foster child, tears glistening in her eyes. "Farewell, son of a King," she said. "I cannot tell you your father's name; it will be shown you before long. When they are ready, I will send your cousins to join you and fight beside you. Do not tarry at the High King's court; the hall is not the place for a warrior. Ride out on the open road and prove your valor in the eyes of men."

So Lancelot rode with Arthur and Gawain to the fortress of Camelot. The last he saw of the woman who had reared him was a shimmer of white in the dusky wood.

As he had promised, the High King knighted the warrior; the Queen herself buckled on his sword. Lancelot trembled at her touch, but he was a young man unused to women, and those who saw the movement smiled, charmed by the shyness.

Wise in enchantment was the fairy named the Lady of the Lake, who hid the French prince Lancelot in his youth and shaped him to be the finest warrior in the world.

Shyness was indeed his feeling at first, but something more happened. Lancelot knelt before the High King and Queen to make his oath of fealty. He asked, as was the custom, if he might serve as the Queen's own knight and liege man, to defend her and take his prizes in her honor. As he made the request, he raised his head to receive the Queen's blessing. The most infinitesimal of pauses followed: Queen and knight gazed upon each other, eye drinking eye as if the souls shone out unmasked. In such an instant had Uther Pendragon seen Igraine of Cornwall; in such an instant had Arthur been caught by Morgause his sister. Yet the look promised more than passion, more than a recognition of desire. A tremor of surprise, a *frisson* of sorrow swiftly disciplined, crossed the Queen's face. She nodded her assent to the formal request and gave Lancelot leave to seek adventure. He went

When he came of age, Lancelot – called du Lac – journeyed from his other-world home

t of Arthur. He was knighted by the High King; Guinevere the Queen girded on his sword.

Lancelot was the most beloved of Arthur's knights
for his defense of his fellows: Again
and again in the course of his adventures he was
their champion in adversity.

from court at once, with only a squire to serve him.

Such journeying was the business of knights in those days: Fighting was the existence they were trained for, and they seemed fully themselves only in combat. They had to test themselves in battle, and test themselves repeatedly, to prove their skills and courage. And there was no lack of fighting. The High King's peace kept Britain whole, but Britain was a different island then, clothed in trackless forests, pocketed with isolated, little-known kingdoms and peoples, laced with the last hidden territories of the old ones. In Britain—as in Flanders, in Brittany, in the French kingdoms— private wars and feuds, some of them savageries lasting for decades, were common. No traveler could tell when he would cross a boundary onto a battlefield and find himself caught in some brutal combat with strangers at his side.

Even sport was training for war.

In every kingdom, no matter how small, tournaments were regularly held, and these tournaments were not the orderly displays of later eras. Except that the dates and places were publicly announced, that areas were set aside where exhausted and wounded knights might withdraw from the lists to rest, and that prizes were awarded to the best fighters, tournaments were indistinguishable from actual battle. Groups of knights, riding in closed formation, charged each other across an open field. When the warriors were unhorsed by the force of the charge, they fought on foot with broadswords. Defeated knights forfeited to their captors all the accouterments they possessed—armor, arms, horse. This was a serious loss indeed, for the arming and mounting of a knight cost as much as a herd of oxen, an enormous sum. Some poorer chevaliers made their fortunes by their prowess, traveling from tournament to tournament, collecting arms that had to be redeemed with gold. Others, like Lancelot and Gawain, fought for the glory and the sheer joy of it.

The chronicles of Lancelot's adventures consist of scattered accounts of battles and of tournaments, vague as to place and time and even as to sequence. Of his earliest journey—before he learned his true name and parentage—it is known that he rode into Northumberland, to find the castle called Dolorous Garde and certain of Arthur's knights who had vanished there.

The journey took him into harsh country, hardly inhabited except for scattered, crumbling villages where wretched folk fell silent at the sight of him; they cringed away from his questions, and if they gave answer at all, it was in frightened mumbles. When at last folk told him that he neared his destination, he left his squire to make camp in a small wood and rode alone across rolling, scrub-covered moors to the place where the castle stood.

At first sight, it seemed a fortress of the dead. Its toothed battlements reared high on an outcropping of rock; sea gulls screamed around the windowless walls, and their harsh cries and the moaning of the wind were the only sounds to be heard. Lancelot paused in a stand of trees to survey the terrain. There seemed to be no way to approach the place unseen.

"It is not for you to approach by stealth," said a voice among the trees. The horse started and sidled nervously; Lancelot held it with an iron hand and looked down. Something moved among the tree trunks, appearing and disappearing, something as silver as birches and brown as the oak. He waited.

"I serve her who guards the Lake and fostered you in your youth," said the fairy woman, settling at last. She was hardly distinguishable from the trees, except for her moving eyes. "She bids me tell you this: Ten knights guard the castle's outer gate and ten knights the inner. Their lord is a copper man. When you have breached the outer gate, the copper lord will fall and the defenders will be at your mercy. I can offer you this: shields to give you magic strength as lasting as your enemies'."

I will fight only with my own strength," said Lancelot. He rode up the rocky road to the castle gate and shouted his challenge. No voice answered, but when he retreated to the plain beneath the road to give himself fighting room, the gate swung open. Swift as the wind, a knight charged, gathering speed from the decline of the road. Lancelot sat unmoving on his white horse. He held his lance steady, braced on his saddle. Its point took the adversary through the slit of his visor, lifting him from his horse. The man's neck cracked as his head struck the ground, and he lay broken at Lancelot's feet. Strangely, there was no sign of blood. But Lancelot had only a moment to register this, for a second knight left the gate and thundered down the stone road toward him.

This knight, too, he slew—or at least vanquished: The body lay motionless beside that of its brother, and no more than its brother did it bleed. The horses of both warriors galloped away across the moors as Lancelot faced his third adversary.

In the years of Arthur's prime, the Round Table of his company was the sign of unity and perfection. And Lancelot du Lac, his premier knight, sat at the High King's right hand.

"They have more than human strength. It is fair that you take my aid," said the voice, and Lancelot leaned from the saddle to accept the silver shield the fairy woman offered. She vanished into a shadow among the bracken, but his attention was elsewhere. At the instant he touched the shield, power had flowed into his arm and the battle fury into his mind. He fought with cold rage, blind to everything except the lances and swords of his enemies, unaware of the passing of the hours or the waning of the light.

The battle ended as suddenly as it had begun. Silence fell again, except for the raucously crying gulls. Around him on the field, ten bodies lay, melting into the earth even as he watched. Above him, the outer gate of the castle stood open, revealing only blackness.

"At first light you will fight at the inner gate," said the voice of the fairy woman. "You will bear a second shield. Rest now, and I will keep watch."

And in the gray dawn, bearing the shield the fairy gave him, Lancelot rode up the hill and through the open portal. In the wide space between the outer and the inner walls of Dolorous Garde ten knights were ranged, faceless men hooded in steel.

Above them, on the archway of the gate, stood a great warrior cast in copper, staring down with sightless copper eyes. The statue leaned as Lancelot watched; it fell, carrying one of his enemies to the ground. Sword in hand, silver shield high, Lancelot charged the others. Those who did not flee he slaughtered.

And when he had finished, the inner gate of Dolorous Garde swung slowly open. The brown and silver fairy woman appeared, hardly more substantial than a shadow. She beckoned him in. Stiffly, limping from a leg wound, he followed, and she showed him how each crenelation of the inner wall bore a helmeted skull. At the base of the wall beneath each skull, a gravestone lay, marked with each dead knight's name. One grave only bore no name, a long marble slab lying flat on the grass. On the stone these words appeared: *This slab will never be raised by hand or strength of man, save only by him that will conquer this dolorous castle, and his name is written beneath.*

"Is this where I will lie?" he said. His companion nodded.

He bent, thrust his hands under the slab and lifted. The marble swung up to show the words carved in its underside: *Here will lie Lancelot du Lac, the son of King Ban of Benwic.*

Thus Lancelot learned of his beginning and his end. If it gave him grief or fear, he did not say so. He went on with his wandering, and Camelot heard many tales of his battles—of giants he had slain, of fellow warriors he had delivered. It was said, for instance, that a knight named Turquin had imprisoned Gaheris, Gawain's brother, as well as Kay, Ector and Lionel; Lancelot fought Turquin alone and beheaded him. Lancelot was a fair fighter and a generous one; those who yielded to him he sent to yield themselves to Guinevere, and so their names were recorded: Gaunter and Gyllymer, Raynold and Pedyvere and Belleus.

And when months or a year or two years had gone by, he himself returned to his King, having proved his worth. He was leaner than he had been. The fresh young skin was drawn and scarred now, and the open glance had become watchful. The white armor was gone, lost in some battle long-forgotten. But Gawain, who had joined him when the paths they wandered crossed, and who loved him with the fierce love of one knight for another, saw the battered figure ap-

Among the enchantments of Morgan le Fay was a shield emblazoned with the figures of king, queen and knight. It revealed the tale of Guinevere and Lancelot, but it was many years before the High King understood its meaning.

proaching on the high road that led to the fortress and called his name: Even from the distance, he knew Lancelot by his riding.

And when he was brought into the hall and met the Queen again, she recognized the same soul she had seen before; one glance alone told that there was no change. Except for that one glance, Lancelot made no move: He had been bred to honor. The High King was his liege lord, and the bond between them the deepest a knight could have. Nor did Guinevere act. She was a King's daughter and wife to a King; the sacredness of royalty clung to her person. She loved her husband, and his honor was hers.

Sometime in the years that followed, however, their vigilance weakened. The stories are so varied and so conflicting that the truth is difficult to determine — and in any case does not matter. Guinevere and Lancelot became lovers and steadfastly and secretly remained lovers for many years. That their liaison went undiscovered for so long was surprising, considering the public nature of life in royal palaces. But it began to come to light eventually: Other eyes than mortal ones watched Arthur's court, eyes that spied for beings eager to destroy Arthur's power. Morgan le Fay, weaving her enchantments in her own spell-misted lands, brooded raven-like, devouring scraps and hints and whispers. When she thought the time was right, she acted.

It happened one year that the High King held his autumn court at London, receiving there his knights returning from their summer forays. One by one, they rode into the city and sat in the King's hall and described their adventures. Gawain was among the last to arrive. On a chill afternoon, the Orkney knight, weatherbeaten and grizzled now, sat at Arthur's hearth fire and told his story to the High King and the Queen. It was a long and rambling narrative, full of tournaments and riding; it ended with a tale of how Gawain had been entrapped by a Prince named Carados, how he had been disarmed and imprisoned in a stone tower in the heart of a forest.

⚜ ⚜ ⚜ ⚜ ⚜ ⚜ ⚜ ⚜ ⚜ ⚜ ⚜ ⚜ ⚜ ⚜ ⚜ ⚜ ⚜

Lancelot had rescued him, killing Carados in his fury and setting Gawain free. It had been a grand battle, Gawain said with a rueful grin; he had watched it from his prison window. He described it in some detail for Arthur. The Queen listened quietly, oblivious to the rain that drummed on the paving stones outside, to the hounds that played in the rushes at her feet, to the pages who scurried to and fro, bearing wine and meat for the traveler. When Gawain finished his tale and paused to drink, she said, "And what of Lancelot?"

"He left me as soon as he saw that I was fit to ride. He told me he was going to a good place. I thought him with the King by now."

If the Queen's heart contracted with impatient longing, she gave no sign: She was used to the separations, and she was a woman of stern discipline. She said merely, "He is not here. We have had no word."

"Well, then it may be that he has ridden to his own lands," said Gawain, without concern. Lancelot, over the years, had regained his father's territories in France, and he had land in Britain, too, for Arthur had bestowed on him the northern fortress he had conquered in his first venture. Lancelot had changed its name to Joyous Garde.

ut Lancelot was not at Joyous Garde, nor was he in France. In the evening, as if timed to Gawain's arrival, a young woman was brought into the hall, a tall, swarthy woman, hooded and cloaked for travel. She stood between two men-at-arms, surveying the company with composure, and Arthur signaled for the men to release her. When they had done so, she said, "Sire, I come from distant lands and I bring strange tidings. Before I speak, I would be assured that I shall receive neither shame nor ill for what I say. There are some my news may offend." Her black eyes flickered toward the Queen.

"Speak," replied the High King. "Never in my court was a messenger harmed for the news he had brought."

"High King, I bring you tidings of Lancelot du Lac. Know that you will nevermore see him in your dwelling, neither you nor any of your fellowship, for he is in a place where he will not easily be found. And even if he were found it would avail nothing, for he will not again carry his shield into battle."

Guinevere rose slowly to her feet and turned to leave. The messenger said, "Sire, if you suffer the Queen to leave, I shall tell no more," and Guinevere stayed as she was, her knuckles white on the arm of her high stool.

"Sir Lancelot was wounded when he left this knight," the woman continued, gesturing at Gawain, who nodded. "The wound festered, and he feared for his life, so he confessed to me the vile sin he had done against his lord. He told me he had betrayed the High King with this lady, the Queen. And he sent this token to the Queen that she might know these words for the truth. The token is one she gave him." She held out her hand; on the palm lay a heavy signet, ornamented with Lancelot's arms. The company stared at it.

❧ ❧ ❧ ❧ ❧ ❧ ❧ ❧ ❧ ❧ ❧ ❧ ❧ ❧ ❧

Releasing her hold on the stool, Guinevere turned to the High King and, in a steady voice, denied the charge. "If I did nothing but recount the noble graces that were in Lancelot," she said, "my tongue would fail before I could finish. He was the fairest and best of all knights; he surpassed them all in valor. But may God have mercy on my soul if Lancelot would not let the eyes be drawn from his head before he would tell the lies this woman has recounted. God and the world know that I have never loved Lancelot nor he me with a base love. But even if it were with us as this woman said, I would not deny the ring, and all who will may blame me for it. I care not; it is blame without support."

A ring of gold adorned with his escutcheon was Lancelot's signet. It was given by the Queen.

Thus Guinevere the Queen forswore her soul before her husband and her people. Arthur believed her, and so he said. The messenger shrugged when she heard the High King's reply. She turned to leave the hall, but Gawain gave an order to the men-at-arms, and they pinned her hands to her sides.

"What master do you serve, woman?" the Orkney knight demanded. "Where have you hidden Lancelot?"

"As to the hiding place, I may not tell it. As to master, I serve my lady, the Queen of Gorre." The men-at-arms made the sign against evil.

"Let her go, she who serves the Queen of Lies," said the High King. He turned to Gawain, the most precious of his warriors after Lancelot. But Gawain—with Yvain and Lionel, Lancelot's cousin—was already striding from the hall, ready to ride in search of his fellow knight.

They searched for long months, but the messages they returned were unencouraging: Lancelot's shield had been found; he himself had been seen, weakened and injured and wandering in his mind; he had vanished again. It was a year before Lancelot returned to the High King, pale and wasted, with a tale of Morgan le Fay, who had imprisoned him with enchantment, drugged him so that she might take the ring from his finger, laid a spell of madness on him and then set him free to wander in the woods.

The Queen wept for his wounds and his struggle to fight free of the charm, and if any thought ill of her for it, none said so. Her people, the chroniclers wrote, loved and honored her for her defense of Lancelot's honor. But it was a false defense, and in the years that followed there were many eyes upon the pair, watching to see how they went on together.

Yet those years were serene and golden. The knights rode out in the summers as they always had done. Lancelot, as he always had, sent his prisoners to surrender in the Queen's name, making honor for her with his prowess. At court, he—with Gawain—was closest to the High King.

In quiet places hidden from the eyes of the High King's court, Lancelot and Guinevere made lovers'
vows, although the words meant dishonor and danger and ruin in the end.

Together as a glorious company, the knights of the Round Table rode out on the venture of the Grail, and the Queen wept to see them go. That was the warriors' last time in unity.

And while people watched the lovers, there were greater matters coming to the fore, in the form of the last great quest of Arthur's company. Word reached the court – in the songs of minstrels, in the reports of wanderers – of a land to the far north that lay under a wasting enchantment because the talisman that protected it had been defiled and the King of the country wounded. Only the perfect knight, perfectly formed for the task, could break the enchantment and restore life to the land.

Different knights attempted the journey. At first word, Lancelot himself made it. He saw the King; he fathered a child on the King's daughter. But he did not see the talisman that was the Grail. His honor was flawed by his liaison with Guinevere, a disloyalty to the High King whom he served. His failure told him what no one knew, that he was not the chosen one, the best knight in the world.

This is the story of Arthur's fate, not of Lancelot's, and the matter of the Grail belongs to other chronicles. It is enough to remember that Lancelot's son, the spotless knight, the younger Lancelot who bore his father's given name – Galahad – came to court when he was old enough; that after his arrival, the Grail itself appeared, floating in the air in Arthur's hall. It is enough to remember the final splendor of the company of Arthur—Lancelot and Lionel and Bors and Gawain and Percival and Galahad and all the rest—as they set out, banners flying, riding north to deliver a kingdom from a curse.

Those who came back were graver men than they had been. They had seen the wonder: how Galahad, the perfect knight, had said the words that freed the Waste Land; how Percival had stayed to rule it in the old King's place; how some knights had died and some gone mad; how Lancelot had failed and was denied the glory, although they could not tell why.

hey came back to create a different court. The younger and the more restless of them began to gather in factions, not openly rebellious yet, but chafing under the High King's rule. There was covert feuding; blood was shed and shed again. The forces that sought King Arthur were gathering and growing as he aged. The weak chink in his armor was the dishonor that he did not know existed—the long love of Lancelot and Guinevere. The weapon the old ones used to pierce that armor was the High King's son by his sister, the child that Arthur and Merlin had sought—vainly and at an awful price in blood—many years before: Mordred of Lothian and Orkney.

❧ ❧ ❧ ❧ ❧ ❧ ❧ ❧ ❧ ❧ ❧ ❧ ❧ ❧ ❧ ❧

VI

⚘MORDRED⚘

he chronicles of the High King's court were sometimes vague about the histories of the sons of Lothian and Orkney. Gawain, of course, was accepted into Arthur's household shortly after the death of Lot and knighted on Arthur's wedding day; throughout his life he stalwartly remained a king's man. Two brothers—Agravain, handsome but of evil disposition, and Gaheris—apparently came with him. Another brother, Gareth, arrived some years later, so anxious to prove his worth that he traveled anonymously and served as a page in the High King's kitchens until he had the chance to show his bravery and skill adventuring. He was famous for his sweet temper.

Shortly after Gareth was knighted, his mother, Morgause, followed him to Camelot, impelled, she claimed, by a desire to see her sons. The young men fell on their knees before her when they understood who she was. They had not seen their mother for fifteen years.

Morgause did not travel alone. It seems that she brought along her youngest child in order to present him to the High King. That child was Mordred, as fine of feature as his mother, and as secretive as she; the two were very close. He was unaware of his true parentage; the name of Lot was often on his lips. If Arthur recognized him for the child he had fathered, he did not say so. Mordred was knighted, as his brothers had been before him, and made one of the company of the Round Table. Gawain kept close to him, as he did to all his brothers. Lancelot, too, watched over the young knight, for Gawain's sake.

Morgause stayed at court, held in honor as the King's sister. Except for Arthur and herself, no one knew of the deed of her youth. She had retained her beauty. The white wings that swept through her dark hair seemed no worse than a crown for her delicate features. Her eyes had not lost their avid shine, nor her voice its seductive charm. Within a few months, she had taken a lover younger than her elder sons— Lamorak of Wales, called the third best knight in Arthur's company, after Lancelot and Tristram of Lyonesse. At tournaments, Lamorak wore her favor—a strip of silk, woven with the double eagle of Lothian and Orkney, streaming from his helmet crest.

⚘ ⚘ ⚘ ⚘ ⚘ ⚘ ⚘ ⚘ ⚘ ⚘ ⚘ ⚘ ⚘ ⚘ ⚘

Her sons were outraged. Descendants of fierce northern tribes, they were not ones to forget a blood feud. Lamorak's father was Pellinore of the Isles, who long years before had slain rebellious Lot in battle. Gawain, no more than a boy then, had sworn vengeance, and he had gained it. Some time after they were knighted, Gawain and Gaheris killed Pellinore in a fight. Now their anger rose again: Their mother shamed them, lying with a man of Pellinore's blood.

The sons of a widow could rule the mother in those days. These sons, led by Gawain, took the matter into their own hands. They removed Morgause from the temptations of the court and established her in a pretty hunting lodge some miles from Camelot. Never given to open conflict, Morgause acquiesced with dignity and sweet smiles, and she praised her sons' solicitude. It was little hardship for her, after all. She had a handsome household and no shortage of messengers to do her bidding.

Within a week, she summoned Lamorak. But Gaheris saw his mother's waiting woman whispering to the Welsh knight in a palace corridor, and when Lamorak rode out from Camelot, he followed, keeping his distance. He arrived at his mother's house in the evening and found her lover's horse tied to the postern gate. Quietly, Gaheris dismounted and moved through the hall, where his mother's serving people slept on pallets by the hearth. He paused at the door that led to his mother's chamber. Lamorak's shield, sword and mail lay on a stool there. Gaheris drew his sword and opened the door.

His mother lay in the great bed, her white face turned toward him, her hair streaming over bare shoulders. With two strides, Gaheris was at her side, hacking at her throat with the sword, screaming in a rage that brought Lamorak to his feet beside the bed. The blood made a fountain that spattered the bedclothes and Lamorak and Gaheris himself. Gaheris straightened, panting and weeping, to face Lamorak across the twitching body.

"Foul and evil, to slay the mother who bore you," the Welsh knight cried. But Gaheris hardly heard these words in his wrath.

"Beware where you meddle," he shouted. "Your father slew our father, and for you to lie beside our mother is too much shame for us to bear. This is the end of her wantonness. Because you are an unarmed man, I will not fight you now. But beware, Lamorak. When you go abroad, my brothers and I will find you." Then Gaheris strode blindly from the chamber, knocking aside the servants huddled at the door.

The reaction at court to the news of Morgause's death was stern, but it was not so intense as it might have been in other, less bloody eras. Gaheris was exiled for a time. Lamorak did not appear; he had ridden, apparently, to his own territory in Wales. But he was a dead man, as Lancelot, having argued in vain with Gawain, told the High King. Within a few months, the brothers—with the exception of Gareth, who would not join them—had found their mother's lover, riding on a lonely road. It was said that Agravain, Gawain, Gaheris and Mordred together challenged him, and he valiantly faced them all. They killed his horse under him; he fought them on foot. He held them off for three hours, so great was his strength. But in the end, Lamorak fell when Mordred circled behind him and stabbed him in the back.

So the feud between the family of Pellinore and that of Lot was ended, it seemed. It was finished by four men fighting one and by a knife in the back – the coward's way. How much of Mordred's part was known at the time is difficult to say. Mordred's reputation was that of a courageous but inexperienced warrior: He had been a knight no longer than two years. The men of the Round Table readily accepted his company on their journeying, if not for himself then for love of his brother Gawain, that doughty lion. Loyalty to Gawain, in fact, saved Mordred from Lancelot once, when Lancelot might have acted against him and thereby altered the pattern of Arthur's fate.

Morgause of Lothian and Orkney was a woman of much appetite and little discretion. In her middle years, she took for a lover Lamorak of Wales, son of the man who slew her husband.

On a May morning a few years after Mordred received the spurs of knighthood, it happened that he and Lancelot set out separately from Camelot to seek trials of their knightly worth. Deep in a wood in Wales their paths crossed. Glad of company in the wilderness, they rode on together, and in the adventures that they had – which do not matter to the story – Mordred distinguished himself by valor and by canny fighting. Lancelot praised him for it, drawing from the younger man an uncommon flush of pleasure. Mordred rarely displayed emotion, which made the events that followed all the more surprising.

By a brook in the wood, a cairn of stones rose – the grave, perhaps, of an ancient,

Gaheris, son of Morgause, found her with Lamorak one night. In a rage of shame tha

...uld so lightly betray his father's memory, the knight put his mother to the sword.

long-forgotten prince. The tomb, it seemed, was guarded. A hut of bent willow branches, such as wood elves sometimes built, rose near it, and by the door of the hut a man sat, nodding in a patch of sun. Elvish he was not: He was bent and old; shaggy white hair hung around his shoulders; and the robes he wore were the tattered rags of the more ascetic of priestly hermits. He appeared to be asleep. When the two men dismounted to water their horses, however, he arose at once and greeted them in a whistling whisper. They courteously told him their names, and he smiled, the seams and creases of his face twisting into a grotesque picture of senile mockery.

"Welcome," he said. "I give welcome to the two most unfortunate knights in the world." He beckoned, and the men, leaving the horses to drink, walked toward him. As they neared, the cracked voice began again, speaking in a rapid, toneless mumble:

"Mordred, you will do great harm. Through you the Round Table will be destroyed. You will kill your own father. Through you, your great heritage will cease to exist."

Lamorak died fighting four of the sons of Morgause. It was Mordred who gave the death blow: a knife in the back.

"This is witless talk, grandfather," Mordred replied. "I cannot kill my father, for he is dead."

But the old one droned on: "King Lot was not your father. Arthur the High King is your father. The night he begat you on Morgause, he dreamed that a serpent issued from him. He killed it. In the dream, he died of its poison. You are that serpent, Mordred, full of evil, without pity. Your father will kill you for it. His spear will pierce your belly, and daylight will show through the wound. After that day, Arthur will be seen no more on earth."

Mordred stared at him.

"And you will kill me," the ancient voice added. So it was. Mordred drew his sword and silenced the old man with one vicious stroke. Mordred wiped his blade on the ragged robe; then he sheathed the weapon and said, "In the midst of lies you told a truth. Kill you I have, grandfather." He glanced up to meet Lancelot's grim gaze.

"For shame, Mordred, to murder an unarmed elder," Lancelot said. His hand was clamped on his own sword hilt. "If it were not for the sake of your brother Gawain, I would kill you where you stand."

But he did not kill Mordred, and he did not speak of the incident. Even later, when Mordred became a deadly threat to him, Lancelot did not speak.

After that day, Mordred went no more adventuring. He spent his time at court, lurking in corners, skulking in stables, watching the movements of Lancelot, who had heard the old man's prophecy. As if driven by fear of its revelation, he set out to destroy the French knight. He had the weapon at hand. Lancelot's devotion to the Queen was of such long standing that few people bothered to comment on it, but Mordred had seen things – perhaps a figure in the window of the Queen's chamber, a glance held too long between the two, the faintest brush of a touch in passing – that told the truth. The two were lovers still. And Mordred talked. He talked to the other knights – cadets, like himself, too young to have seen the glories of Arthur's prime, who chafed at the old ways of the court. And he talked to his brothers, patiently, over and over, whispering of Lancelot's dishonor and of the cuckolding of the High King. He spoke of the Queen, too, and the words he used were ugly ones. The Queen was sacred. In her person, as in that of the High King, resided the health of Britain, people thought. Her betrayal of the High King's bed was treason, endangering the kingdom.

The brothers' reactions were characteristic: Gawain told Mordred to hold his tongue, and after a while he kept apart from him so that he might not see Mordred's significant looks or hear his tales of evidence, found by hiding in shadows and listening at windows. Gareth ignored him. But hot-tempered Gaheris and Agravain, sour of nature and envious of disposition, listened. And they, too, talked.

So a miasma, a cloud of spiteful rumor, spread through the corridors and chambers of Camelot, infecting all it touched. Quarrels broke out, for Lancelot's cousins fiercely defended him, and there were many who still loved the Queen and were prepared to fight in the name of her honor. As for Guinevere, when the whispers reached her ears, she kept apart from her lover for a while. But to see Lancelot always at a distance, never to lie with him in the secret night, never to speak, except in the company of others, brought only suffering to the Queen. She sent Lancelot away from court.

Then, brave and gallant woman that she was, Guinevere summoned the gossips to her chambers and offered them a feast. The sons of Lothian and Orkney were there, and nineteen other knights, some of them grave and silent, some sullen, some almost leering. Guinevere welcomed them and gave her hand to each man in turn. And in turn, each man knelt and kissed it, as he was bound to do in homage. When they had all given her the honor that was her due, Guinevere signaled. Music began, and

From an aged stranger, Mordred learned that he was no true son of Lot. The High King was Mordred's father, and he himself
was the serpent who would take his father's life. Mordred slew the messenger. Lancelot saw him do it.

pages trooped to the long board, bearing laden silver platters, ivory jugs filled with wine, and dishes of apples as a compliment to Gawain. Lot's eldest son was known for his love of the fruit.

It seemed that the Queen's grace would put an end to the talk. But partway through the meal, a knight named Patrise of Ireland lurched to his feet and stood swaying, gurgling wordlessly while his face swelled and blackened and his eyes started from his head. Then he pitched forward onto the table, smashing into the food platters and knocking over the wine. His hand clenched in his death agony and then opened, and a half-eaten apple rolled onto the cloth.

A crack of maniacal laughter sounded. "Fine food you give your people, lady," said Mordred. Gawain silenced him, but his face was sad and tired. Speaking for the company, Gawain told the Queen to guard herself. She had offered poisoned apples to those who doubted her, he said, and a man had died because of it. There would be vengeance to pay. Then he led his companions from the room.

There was vengeance to pay indeed. Patrise's cousin, Mador de la Porte, accused the Queen to Arthur and demanded that her guilt be determined in the customary way: In his dead cousin's name, he would fight any man who chose to defend the Queen's innocence. Arthur heard him out. He himself could not fight for Guinevere because he was the High King and because she was his wife. He knew her to be innocent: Guinevere was no murderess. But being a just man, he agreed to the trial by combat, and he called for a knight to defend the Queen.

Not one stepped forward. Lancelot was gone from court and nowhere to be found. Not one man, it seemed, believed enough in the Queen's innocence to risk his life against the skill of Mador. Perhaps it was then, when the wife he honored was denied honor, that Arthur sensed the net of fate begin to draw in around him. He sent for Bors, Lancelot's cousin, and himself asked that Bors duel on behalf of the Queen. Bors said he could not; he had been at the dinner, and his fellow knights would suspect him of complicity.

In the end, the Queen, reduced to pleading, begged Bors on her knees to stand for her. Her own knight, Lancelot, was gone, she knew not where. If Bors had even a doubt of her guilt, she said, he must defend her.

Bors pulled her to her feet, horrified at her humiliation. "Madam," he said, "you do me dishonor." But he weakened. He agreed to stand as the Queen's champion unless a better knight than he appeared.

And when his fellows cried out against him and called the Queen a destroyer of knights, steadfast Bors replied that there had been murder done, but the Queen had not done it. "As far as I could know, she was a maintainer of knights," Bors said. "She has been generous and free with her possessions to all good knights, and the most bounteous lady in her gifts and her good grace that I ever saw or heard speak of, and

*A dish of apples presented at a royal
feast contained poison that murdered an innocent knight.
Guinevere the Queen was the
poisoner, said the sons of Lothian and Orkney.*

so I shall prove with my body."

On the appointed day, then, the court gathered at a tournament ground at Winchester. Mador de la Porte, his shield on his shoulder and his lance in his hand, rode to King Arthur and shouted, "Bid your champion come forth if he dares." Bors rode slowly to one end of the lists.

Before the heralds could cry the start, however, another knight galloped onto the field. He was armored in white and his visor was down, hence none could read his device or see his face. He brought his horse around beside Bors and said formally, "Fair knight, I pray you be not displeased, for here must a better knight than you have battle. Therefore I pray you withdraw. I have had this day a great journey, and this battle ought to be mine. It is a dishonor to the High King and to all the knights of the Round Table that so noble and courteous a lady as Queen Guinevere should be rebuked and shamed among you."

"I am discharged, then," Bors replied without expression. He left the field to the cousin he himself had sent for.

The adversaries turned and couched their lances to face each other down the lists. When they thundered together, Mador broke his lance, but the other man's weapon held, knocking Mador and his horse to the ground. "Oh, well ridden," said Gawain suddenly to the King. "It is Lancelot; I know his style."

A skillful fighter, Mador extricated himself from the tangle of horse and harness in short order, drawing his sword as he surged to his feet, shouting for his adversary to dismount and face him. Lancelot did that, and the two men swung into the ponderous and deadly dance of broadsword battle, "rushing and crossing, slashing and thrusting, and crashing together" – the chroniclers wrote – "like wild boars." They fought for an hour, until Mador was knocked to the earth. Lancelot moved in, but Mador was on his feet again, dealing a great, slashing stroke to the thigh. And when Lancelot felt the blood rush out, his battle fury came upon him. He hit Mador so violently on the helmet that the man was knocked flat. In an instant, Lancelot's hand

On her knees, Guinevere pleaded for a knight to defend her innocence in a trial by combat. Bors, cousin to Lancelot du Lac, was the only man willing to stand for her.

Shades of evil began to close in on the High King of Britain. Morgan le Fay showed him
the intrigues of Guinevere and Lancelot, painted on a chamber wall.

was on the helmet, to free the head for the death blow. But Mador cried mercy and asked for his life. He yielded up his charge against the Queen.

The Queen's innocence was held proved by Lancelot's victory, but it was proved again, when the true poisoner confessed. His had been another move – the last – in the feud between the sons of Pellinore and the sons of Lot. A knight called Sir Pyonel le Savage, cousin to Lamorak, had poisoned the apples, hoping to kill Gawain in revenge for Lamorak's death. When Gawain heard this news he sighed, but he said to his brothers, "Now you know of the innocence of our lady Queen. So shut your whispering and your gossip."

But Agravain – the chroniclers called him Sir Agravain the Open-mouthed – snapped, "Innocent of murder, yes. But Lancelot lies nightly with the Queen, and it is a shame to us that we let the King be so dishonored. We must tell him of the evil that is daily done him."

"You have been listening to Mordred, fool," said Gawain. "Cease your talking, I say. I do not believe you, and I will not be party to your plotting, brother or no."

"Nor I," said Gaheris.

"Nor I," said Gareth. "I will speak no evil of the man who made me a knight."

"I will," said Mordred softly.

awain swung on him. "Aye, Mordred, I believe you well. Ever to all evil will you agree. You forget – and you, Agravain – how often Lancelot has defended both King and Queen and how he has stood beside you in battles you were not skilled enough to win. For my part, I will never be against Sir Lancelot, for that he saved my life. And I tell you, you will destroy the kingdom if you go on with your talk."

"Befall what may befall," replied Agravain with a shrug. "I will tell the King indeed." And Mordred smirked in assent. Gawain looked long and hard at him. Then, with Gareth and Gaheris at his heels, he left the courtyard.

So Agravain and Mordred asked for privy conference with the High King. He received them in a tower chamber, bare except for piles of shields and swords, and as they talked, he stared out the open window at the silver river that wound past Camelot, at the fields that flanked the river, at the rich forests that lay beyond.

Agravain laid the family quarrel before him. He said in tones of piety, "My lord, I may keep it no longer. I and my brother Mordred are your sister's sons, and we may suffer this outrage no more. Sir Lancelot holds the Queen and has long done so. We all know that he is a traitor, and we will furnish proof of it."

The High King did not reply at once. He continued to look upon the rich and peaceful countryside, golden, waiting for the harvest. He had heard those pious tones weeks before, from his sister Morgan le Fay. She had appeared in his track one evening when he rode out alone; she had begged his forgiveness; she had led him into a little lodge that lay hidden in the forest, and there she had shown him walls painted with scenes of Lancelot and Guinevere walking alone in a wood, lying in a field of flowers beside a stream, entering a chamber where a great bed stood. He had said nothing about it, nothing of the nights filled with bitter imaginings that followed the meeting, nothing of the sorrow and the love he felt for his wife and for the finest of his warriors. It came to him that the old ones had made their final move. Now the magic that they used was no longer needed. The fate that had been woven would be tightened by human hands.

Arthur said, "You speak foul treason, and you speak without proof."

"We will furnish proof," said Mordred.

The High King regarded him with cold eyes, and at last told what he knew. "You are the son of my body, Mordred," he said, "sent to destroy what I have made. I warn you, you will find Lancelot resolute." Then he left them.

But that could not be the end of the matter. By the law, if treason were charged, it must be investigated and, if proved, it must be punished. He himself, the embodiment of the law, could not flout the rule. If he did that, his own justice was dead.

On the morning of the next day, he took a small party and rode out into the mountains to hunt. On the night of that day, Lancelot walked through the darkened lanes of Camelot to meet his lover. Guinevere welcomed him as she had many times before. She drew him into her firelit chamber and bolted the door behind him; she took his cloak and sword from him and laid them aside; she spoke with him of indifferent matters as old lovers do, but she sparkled with all the pleasure of a young bride and laughed aloud for delight at his presence.

Even as they spoke, fists pounded the door and voices called for the death of Lancelot the traitor knight and of Guinevere the false Queen. The two stood motionless, trapped in that instant. Then Guinevere said, "This is the end of our long love."

Lancelot looked about him for armor and shield. There were none; the Queen kept no weapons in her chamber. The pounding at the door ceased for a moment, then resumed, more heavily and rhythmic. Something was being used as a battering ram. He put his arm around the Queen, speaking quickly. "You have always been my good lady," he said. "And I have never failed you since the first day the High King made me a knight. If I fall, pray for me. Whatever comes to me, seek shelter with my kinsman Bors. He and the others will deliver you from death, and they will see that you live as a queen upon my lands."

She shook her head, but she smiled at him in her old way, and Lancelot said, "I would rather have my armor than be lord of all Christendom, so that men might speak of my deeds after I was slain." He picked up his sword. "Lady, take heart," he said. "Since the day has come that our love must end, I shall sell my life as dearly as I can." He turned to the door and shouted, "Lords, leave off your noise. I will open the door. Then you may do with me what you please."

≈ ≈ ≈ ≈ ≈ ≈ ≈ ≈ ≈ ≈ ≈ ≈ ≈ ≈ ≈

Lancelot and Guinevere made their last tryst in the Queen's tower. But Mordred's people lay in wait to prove the lovers' treachery.

Harsh pounding on the chamber door and triumphant shouts in the corridor signaled the entrapment o

rs. Lancelot, unarmored, acted with a warrior's cunning: He let one man only enter and killed him on the spot.

Armored in the dead man's mail, Lancelot slew the warriors who sought his life — all save Mordred, who ran away. Then Lan

…led from Camelot, but Guinevere would not go: Honor demanded that she face the husband whose love she had betrayed.

Burning was the punishment for a traitor Queen,
said Mordred, and saw with satisfac-
tion Guinevere chained to her funeral pyre.

The rhythmic hammering stopped. Something crashed onto the stone stairs outside the door, and Agravain's voice shouted, "Open then! It avails you nothing to fight against the fourteen of us. We will spare your life until you are taken before the High King."

At that instant, Lancelot unbarred the door and held it cracked with his left hand so that only one knight might enter. An arm reached through the crack. He seized it and pulled the man into the room, slamming the door behind. Then he turned to face the man. He was a knight called Colgrevaunce of Gorre; he struck at Lancelot, but Lancelot stepped lightly aside and brought his blade down, knocking the warrior's helmet from his head. Colgrevaunce crumpled to the floor, killed by the force of the stroke. At once, Lancelot turned to Guinevere, and without a word she came to him. Together they unlaced the armor from the body of Colgrevaunce, and Guinevere helped her lover to arm, as she had done years before, in their youth.

The deed was done while the enemies screamed and pounded at the door, and when it was finished, Lancelot cried out, "Sirs, leave your noise. Understand, Agravain, you shall not imprison me this night. If you have wisdom, you will leave the door now and let me go. I swear by my knighthood that if you depart I will appear tomorrow before you and the High King. Then I will know which of you accuses me of treason, and I shall answer you as a knight. I came to the Queen with no evil intent. And that I shall prove on your bodies with my hands."

"We will take you and slay you if we wish," came the answer. "For understand, we have the choice from the King, to spare you or slay you."

"It is a lie," shouted Lancelot. "If there is no other grace in you than lying, guard yourselves." He threw open the door and in an instant was among them, his blade whistling in the air. The first blow killed Agravain the Open-mouthed. And then Lancelot slew the rest—Mador de la Porte, Gyngalyn, Melyot de Logres, Petipace of

Winchelsee, Galleron of Galway, Melyon of the Mountayne, Ascamore, Gromerson Erioure, Cursesalyne, Florence, Lovell – all of them Scots, all of them companions of Mordred. Only Mordred escaped: He took a wound from Lancelot and fled.

Standing triumphant among the bodies, Lancelot entreated the Queen to come with him. She refused. She would not leave the High King, she said. But she added with a smile, "If you have word tomorrow that they will put me to death, you may rescue me as you think best."

"While I am living, I will rescue you," said Lancelot. He kissed her and was gone, leaving her to wait in the bloody chamber.

Before long, Arthur's men-at-arms appeared and dragged the bodies out of the chamber and down the stairs. They told Guinevere that the High King had ordered her arrest. Then they shut the chamber door. She heard their spear butts strike the stone as they settled at their posts.

In the morning, Arthur's company gathered in the High King's hall. They found their numbers much decreased. Bors had gone with Lancelot, as well as Lionel, Ector de Maris and twenty-one others. They had been mounted and waiting, the gate guards said, when Lancelot left the Queen's chamber, having been warned by the fighting at the tower. Someone else said no, they had been warned by a dream that Bors had had. In any case, it was Lancelot they followed, not the High King. The Round Table was broken.

Mordred, even more white-faced than usual from loss of blood, heavily bandaged but still in his armor, brushed this impatiently aside. "The woman must die for the treason," he said. His voice was shrill; his eyes glittered. "She must die by the fire." It was true, and all of them knew it. So sacred was the person of the Queen that if she were slain for treason, danger would cling to her dead body; she must therefore be reduced to ashes that could be carried away by the wind.

"Faugh!" said Gawain. "You are bloodthirsty enough for one who ran away from a fight." He turned to the High King and continued in his slow and earnest way. "My lord Arthur, do not be hasty. Delay the judgment of my lady the Queen. She is beholden to Lancelot, who defended her when no other man would take her part. It is true he went to her chamber, but it may be she sent for him with good intent and with no evil purpose, to thank him for his deeds. I daresay that your lady the Queen is to you both good and true. And as for Sir Lancelot, I daresay he will make it good on any knight living who accuses him of treason and villainy."

"So he will," replied the King. "He can trust in his matchless might and fear no man. But the Queen will die. And if I capture Lancelot, he will die, as it says in the law."

"May I never see it," the old knight replied.

"Gawain, what is this? You have no cause to love Sir Lancelot. Last night he slew your brother Agravain, and almost slew your brother Mordred. And two of the other men he slew were your sons."

Like a wolf of the mountains, Lancelot attacked the crowd that
surrounded Guinevere, the condemned Queen. Two
unarmed men died by his swift hand, although he did not know it.
They were Gareth and Gaheris of Lothian and Orkney.

"My lord," said Gawain, "I know it, and it grieves me. But I told my brothers and my sons beforehand what would happen, and inasmuch as they would not act by my counsel, I will take no revenge for their deaths, which they brought upon themselves." He crossed his arms on his broad chest and stared stubbornly at Arthur.

So Guinevere was judged by the High King and condemned. When the day came, a pyre was made in the great courtyard of the palace. In the hall, Arthur turned to Gawain and asked that the brothers of Lothian and Orkney escort his wife to the place of burning to hear her judgment and receive her death. Gawain refused for himself; he would have none of the judgment of the death, he said. Mordred, he added, with a sneer, was too weak from his wound to attend. Gareth and Gaheris, junior as they were, must obey the High King's command if he made it, but they would not wish to see the shameful deed.

"Sir," said Gareth, "we will go if you command it, but it is against our will. If we go, we go unarmed and unarmored."

"Then, go. Make you ready, for the thing will soon be done," said the High King. Gawain, his face a mask of sorrow and pain, left the hall.

In the courtyard, many of the onlookers wept openly, but Guinevere did not weep. She walked, pale and straight, between her guards. At their command, she stood quiet while her ladies stripped away her veil and unbound her hair. Next, they removed her cloak and overdress and underdress, until she stood before her judges clad only in a white shift. She did not resist when they lifted her onto the pile of fagots. She even raised her arms to take the chains that would bind her to the stake.

Just then, a wild bugle sounded, echoing high and clear over the roofs and around the towers. Huge on their great horses, a host of warriors descended on the courtyard, blades flashing, voices loud in their battle cries. In the fore could be seen the white horse and armor and red-and-silver-blazoned shield of Lancelot du Lac.

The fight was over in moments. Most of the people present were unarmed, as Gareth and Gaheris were, and put up little resistance. Lancelot rode away with Guinevere sheltered in his arms, her shining hair streaming out behind. The warriors left behind a pavement littered with wounded and dying. Among them were Gareth and Gaheris, their heads split open to the chin.

When Sir Gawain saw his brothers, he raised his hands to heaven and gave a howl of grief, quickly stilled. "Who did this?" he cried. And a page told him Lancelot had killed the young men where they stood.

"I will not believe it," Gawain said. "Lancelot would not kill an unarmed man."

"Lord, I myself saw it."

Then Gawain turned to the High King and said, "Lord, now prepare yourself for war. Lancelot killed my young brothers, who always stood by him, and they were unarmed. Now he is my family's enemy. I will pursue the man, and I shall never fail until one of us has slain the other."

❧ ❧ ❧ ❧ ❧ ❧ ❧ ❧ ❧ ❧ ❧ ❧ ❧ ❧ ❧ ❧

In the arms of Lancelot, Guinevere fled the fortress of the High King, riding to the shelter of Joyous Garde.

Robed in white and gold, Lancelot surrendered his lover to Arthur, while Gawain watched and thought of vengeance.

Thus was declared the war that would rend the kingdom Arthur had made and destroy the finest knights in the world. With Gawain at his side, Arthur led a great army north to Joyous Garde, where Lancelot had taken Guinevere and the knights that had flocked to his side. They besieged the castle for fifteen weeks.

Lancelot held out against them. The chroniclers' records of the siege are a collection of brief, sad anecdotes – of angry parleying between Gawain on the ground and Lancelot on the ramparts, of sorties from the castle and furious battles in its shadow. In these battles, Lancelot refused to encounter the High King whom he had served. It was said that Bors once struck Arthur from his horse with a lance. Having the advantage, he drew his sword to strike off Arthur's head and shouted to Lancelot, "Sir, shall I put an end to this war?" But Lancelot forbade the killing. He himself dismounted and saw that Arthur was horsed again. The courtesy brought tears to the High King's eyes. But Gawain was at his right hand, murderous, implacable. No courtesy would ease his rage for vengeance.

Week after week, the bloody, futile siege dragged on. Word of Britain's misery spread across the English Channel, the chroniclers wrote, and reached the ears of the Pope in Rome. He put an end to the fighting for that time: He sent his bishops to the High King and to Lancelot, threatening interdiction on the realm if Guinevere were not restored to the King in safety and if the fighting did not stop.

"She may come back, for aught I care," said Gawain, when he heard of the judgment that had been brought by the bishops. "But the murderer must go. I will kill him if I can, for the sake of my young brothers."

So, on a spring day, the Queen's procession wound across the countryside to the High King's fortress at Carlisle. Lancelot brought Guinevere home with all that was her due. A hundred knights, liveried in green and carrying green branches to signify peace, rode in her train. Beside her, Lancelot sat on his white horse, and both Queen and knight were clothed in white and gold. At the entrance to the hall, Lancelot dismounted and helped Guinevere from her horse; he led her through the ranks of waiting courtiers to Arthur's throne, and he kneeled beside her before the High King. Then he raised her and spoke for them both. For her safety, he declared her innocence; then he told the High King of his own devotion. He spoke of the battles he had fought beside Arthur and his companion Gawain, of the fellowship he had served so long. His words fell into a hush, painting again the picture of the High King's company when it was at its zenith, making his bid for peace.

But these words had no effect on Gawain, who stood beside the High King. He said to Lancelot, "The King may do as he will. But understand, sir, you and I shall never again be in accord while we live, for you slew my brothers treacherously and pitilessly, and they unarmed and unarmored, and I shall kill you for it."

"I would they had been armed, for then they would still be alive. Gawain, I slew your brothers all unknowing. I did not see them in the fray. You know I loved Sir Gareth better than my own kin; it was I who knighted him. I will bewail his death all my life, and not from fear of you, but because of his valor and devotion. And I will do this, Gawain, in his name and for the sake of peace: I will walk barefoot, in my shirt, from Sandwich to Carlisle. Every ten miles I shall endow a convent, where masses will be said for Sir Gareth and Sir Gaheris, to redress the wrong."

A murmur ran through the hall at the offer from the proud knight. But Gawain said, "I never will forgive my brothers' deaths, and if my Uncle, the High King, should accord with you, he will lose my service." He turned his face away. Lancelot waited. At last, the High King shook his head, refusing the fealty of the man who had served him so long.

Lancelot made his departure with formal grace. He kissed the Queen and placed her hand in her husband's. He said for all to hear, "Madam, now I must depart from you and from this noble fellowship forever. And since it is so, I beseech you to pray for me, and I shall pray for you. And if ever you are hard beset by false tongues, send word, my good lady. If any knight's hand may deliver you by battle, it shall be mine."

Guinevere made no reply. She stood motionless by the throne as Lancelot strode from the High King's hall. All his green-clad knights marched with him, away from Arthur, heading for Lancelot's lands in France. Mordred gave a white-lipped smile.

❧ ❧ ❧ ❧ ❧ ❧ ❧ ❧ ❧ ❧ ❧ ❧ ❧ ❧ ❧ ❧

VII

GAWAIN

In the months that followed the exile of Lancelot, the armies of the High King gathered. From Caerleon, from Camelot, from Bedegraine, from Camelerd, from Lyonesse and Tintagel, the vassals of Arthur and his men came, obeying, as they must, the summons of their overlords. Led by marshals bearing the banners of those overlords, long lines of cavalry snaked across the countryside of Britain. Knights, each preceded by the squire who bore his armor, made up the van. They were followed by lesser horsemen, by companies of bowmen, by trains of pack mules carrying supplies. They converged at Cardiff on the Welsh shore and erected bright tents near the High King's castle. Close by, a hundred ships floated at anchor. The King himself rode among the companies, the golden crowns of his standard snapping in the sharp wind that blew off the water. But Arthur moved silently, cloaked in solitude in the midst of the crowd, his face drawn, his eyes hooded. The orders came from the two men who rode at his side, under the double eagle of Lothian and Orkney: Gawain, impatient, burning with barely restrained fury; Mordred, pale of face and always smiling, telling coarse jokes that the soldiers loved.

Mordred remained in Britain, standing as regent for his father. In their armada, the High King's host sailed at last down the Bristol Channel, around the grassy headlands of Lyonesse and across the sea to France. There the armies swept across the fields and through the forests, burning crops and trees as they went, until they reached the high-walled fortress town of Benwic, stronghold of Lancelot. They pitched camp on the plain that lay before the castle; in full view of its towers, they threw up earthworks and built the ladders and the platforms — siege machines — that they would use to scale the walls.

But no response came from Benwic. The sentries paced the walls and did not answer the taunts from Arthur's camp. The iron gates of the town remained barred.

After some days, however, the gates creaked open. A young woman, escorted by a dwarf bearing the white banner of truce, rode down the track that descended from castle to plain. A knight named Sir Lucan le Butler took the reins of the woman's

Commanded by Gawain, the High King's armies sailed for France in pursuit of Lancelot.

palfrey and led her through the crowded camp, among tents and tethered horses, past idle soldiers who gambled with knucklebones on the ground, to the tent crowned with the High King's standard. Arthur sat at its entrance; Gawain stood close by, along with Lucan's brother Bedevere, an old warrior and a steadfast companion to the High King, although he had wept at the departure of Lancelot months before.

The maiden gave Lancelot's offer of peace: that he would remain here on his French lands; that Arthur should cease his attack and return to his own country.

"The offer is a fair one," said Bedevere. "I have no stomach for the death of such as Lancelot."

The High King nodded. But Gawain glared down at the messenger with the flat and lightless eyes of madness. Spittle flecked his grizzled mustache, and his big-veined hands trembled. He swung around to the King. "What will you do, my lord, my Uncle?" he said. "Will you turn back and let the whole world cry villainy and shame, now that you have passed thus far upon your journey?"

"Aye," said Arthur slowly. "I have come on a long journey." He paused, sunk in sadness. Then he said, "I will do as you advise, Gawain, since honor demands it. But it goes against my heart; you must speak the word."

And the son of Lot spoke to the messenger in harsh and grating tones: "Lady, say you to Sir Lancelot that he wastes his breath to appeal now to the High King, my Uncle. And say that I, Sir Gawain, send him word that for the murder of my brothers I will have my revenge. I shall never leave until I have slain him or he me."

The knights around the High King muttered; the maiden left the camp with her message. And during the watches of the night, Arthur's forces prepared for war, heaving ladders to the walls of Benwic, massing below in close-drawn ranks. When they were assembled, Gawain signaled the marshals to hold them in position. Alone, he rode to the castle gates, a huge and menacing figure in his battered armor. He shouted Lancelot's name. Above his head, the soldiers made room to let Lancelot face his old companion. The French knight's kinsmen stood by his side.

"Where are you now, false traitor knight, hiding within holes and walls like a coward? Come out and I shall avenge on your body the deaths of my brothers." Thus Sir Gawain screamed the challenge direct. Above him, the kinsmen of Lancelot waited, grim-faced. By the code bred into the warrior's soul, Lancelot had no choice but to fight. Not to do battle after Gawain's accusations was to admit them and lose all honor. And so Lancelot understood: He said to his fellows that sorrow hung on him at Gawain's words. He told them he knew that now he must fight against the friend of his youth.

He raised his voice, so that his enemies might hear him: "My lord Arthur, noble King that made me knight," he cried. "I am sad for your sake that you strive against me. I have borne it too long, and I will endure it no more. Sir Gawain has called me coward and traitor. It is greatly against my will that I should fight against a man of your blood. But I am driven to it, like a beast at bay."

"Shut your babbling," Gawain snarled. "Come out and let us ease our hearts."

A pause followed, while Gawain withdrew from the gate to the plain below. Soldiers cleared ground for the battle; heralds rode to and fro, establishing the terms: that no warrior come near either combatant to defend or to attack; that the armies refrain from fighting, until Gawain or Lancelot had died or had yielded.

Then the garrison of Benwic left the castle, a mighty troop. Lancelot had indeed endured. His forces were as strong as Arthur's. They ranged their horses along one side of the tilting field that Arthur's soldiers had cleared; motionless as statues, they faced the ranks of Arthur's knights across the great empty space. Gawain took his place at one end of the field. Alone, astride a white charger harnessed in silver, Lancelot du Lac trotted to the other end of the lists. In the breathing hush, a herald cried the start, and the two men couched their lances.

hen they thundered together, lances met shields and shattered harmlessly. So great was the impact, however, that the horses fell injured to the ground. With snorts and whinnies, they rolled free of their riders and trotted off the field. In moments, both knights were on their feet, swords drawn, shields at their shoulders.

Gawain fought with wanton rage, but he had more even than that: It was peculiar to his nature—a gift from some old god, perhaps—that his strength increased as the sun climbed toward noon and decreased after that. So terrible were his rushes, so swift his feints, so savage his strokes, that he could not be touched. Lancelot, cunning warrior that he was, fought defensively then. He "tracked and traversed,"

wrote the chroniclers, covering himself with his shield, saving his strength and making Gawain work for every blow. And shortly after noon, when the sun began its slow descent, Gawain's power began to leave him. He faltered, and Lancelot moved in.

"Now, sir," Lancelot shouted, his voice muffled to a hoarse whisper by his visor. "Much have I endured and will return." He swung: The sword blade glanced off Gawain's quickly upturned shield. He swung again, and the sword crashed into Gawain's helmet, sending Gawain to the ground. He lay, coughing blood, easy prey for his adversary. Lancelot lowered his sword and withdrew to the edge of the lists.

"Why withdraw?" cried Gawain. "Turn back and slay me, for if I recover, you will die by my hand."

"I will fight you, Gawain," Lancelot replied. "I will not strike you as you lie in the dirt." And he limped toward his own ranks, where a squire stood holding his horse for him. Soldiers came onto the field and carried Gawain to the High King's tent.

For three weeks, the uncertain truce held — three long weeks while, in fortress and camp alike, knights and soldiers idled and quarreled among themselves without much energy, three weeks while the physicians worked on Gawain's wound. The defeat and

the humiliation of Lancelot's prowess and of his charity did nothing to the Scots knight's determination. As soon as he could sit a horse, he stood before the gates of Benwic, shouting his challenges again. Again Lancelot met him. Again the two great paladins charged down the lists. The point of the French knight's lance lodged in Gawain's armor; the force of the charge lifted his body from the saddle and his horse's hoofs from the ground. Both fell; Gawain lurched to his feet, shouting curses, and Lancelot dismounted to meet his broadsword.

Again they fought through the morning, in a slow and vicious dance. And again, after the sun had reached its apogee and begun its descent, Gawain faltered, and Lancelot struck him on the helmet, knocking his head to one side and opening the old wound. Gawain slumped unconscious.

Lancelot waited, panting and leaning on his sword. Within moments, Gawain stirred, kicking feebly and waving his arms. "Traitor, I am not yet slain; come now and finish the fight," he cried.

Lancelot, however, stayed as he was, looking down at his adversary. When he spoke, his voice was calm: "I will do no more than I have done," he said. "When I see you on foot, I will battle you, Gawain, and I will fight you as long as you can stand on your

While Arthur and his company did battle in France, Mordred, his traitor son, claimed the High Kingship of Britain and demanded the hand of his father's wife in marriage.

feet." He left the field, with Gawain's voice feebly shouting curses at his back.

So the siege dragged on. Lancelot kept to his stronghold, and no word came from him. Gawain lay in Arthur's tent as before, recovering. When he reached the point where he could sit, he began to talk of fighting Lancelot once more. But a messenger came into the tent, and his words stopped all talk of the duel.

he messenger was a small, lean man, covered with the grime of travel and stinking of horse sweat. He saluted Arthur and handed the High King a folded letter that bore the King's own seal. Then he drank thirstily of the ale that was brought while Arthur read the letter and Gawain dozed. When the King had finished, he said to the messenger, "Is it true what I read here? What more can you tell?" His voice was cold and flat; at its tone, Gawain became alert.

"Sire, it is true. Mordred went among the people and among the knights who were left with him and swore he had letters that said you were dead and named him King. He is a wily man, King. I believed him myself, though your lady said he lied and sent me to you."

"And the Queen?"

"Sire, she was safe at the last word. Sir Mordred said she must marry him because she is the Queen. He could not reign without her. And he told the soldiers that he wanted her. She agreed to all he said, then she fled to London with her household and barricaded herself in the tower there. She cannot hold out long, lord. Sir Mordred and all his host were riding for the city when I left, seven nights ago."

"Gods!" said Gawain from his pallet. "To lust for the wife of his father. My brother is a devil." He gave a child's wail, a cry that came from his weakness and pain, and he added, "It was my rage that brought us to this pass." But only the messenger was there to hear him, to see the madness clear from his eyes, replaced by sorrow. The High King had left the tent, shouting orders.

The camp was struck; the siege on Benwic lifted; the army of the High King rode for the coast of France. Now Arthur was in command, with Bedevere and Lucan beside him. Toward the rear of the great column, Gawain followed, carried on a horse litter.

As the ships of the High King neared Dover, it became apparent that the messenger had been right about Mordred's power. Along the high, white cliffs, bowmen were ranged. The beaches below, where the banner of the double eagle fluttered, were black with horsemen whose body armor glittered in the sun. Warships guarded the shore: Mordred, a man whose spies ranged everywhere, had received word of his father's attack. He sought to prevent Arthur from landing on his own soil.

He failed. In the shallows, on the beaches, the battle was fought. It was led by the High King. In his battle fury, Arthur was a terrifying sight. The men flocked to him, driving Mordred's forces back until finally they broke ranks and fled, scrambling up the cliff paths, leaving their dead behind them on the blood-reddened sand.

As he lay dying from his wounds on the embattled
shore of Britain, Gawain wept for the woe his anger had wrought.

Then quiet fell, except for the moans of the injured and the cries of the curlews circling overhead. Arthur's ships were beached. He walked among them, wading through the shore foam, searching for his dead, rallying the wounded.

He found Gawain lying crumpled among the wooden beams of a small galley, half-hidden by the rowing benches. The Scots knight was alone. His face was ashen; his eyes were closed; his hair and whiskers were matted with the blood from his thrice-wounded skull. He opened his eyes when the High King called his name. But he did not speak until the King's squires had carried him to shore and set him gently on a patch of grass above the filthy sand. He licked his lips then, and Arthur bent to listen.

"This is my death day," Gawain said. He paused, gathering strength to breathe, and the High King replied, "In your person and in Sir Lancelot's, I had my greatest trust. Now I have lost my joy in you both."

ait, Uncle," Gawain whispered. "Through me and my pride you have all this shame and trouble. If Lancelot had been with you — as he would have but for me — this wicked war would never have begun. Of all this sorrow, I am the cause." He requested paper and ink and a quill for writing; and from some messenger's saddle-bag, these were brought. Then Arthur propped the old knight in his arms, and Gawain wrote a letter that the chroniclers, struck by its gallantry, preserved, a letter in the language of chivalry, whose heartbreaking words still echo across the centuries:

Unto thee, Sir Lancelot, flower of all noble knights that I ever heard of or saw in my day, I, Sir Gawain, King Lot's son of Orkney, sister's son unto the noble King Arthur, send greetings, letting thee have knowledge that on the tenth day of May I was smitten upon the old wound that thou gavest me before the city of Benwic; and through that wound I have come to my death day. And I wish all the world to know that I, Sir Gawain, knight of the Round Table, sought my death, which comes not through your fault but by my own seeking. Wherefore I beseech thee, Sir Lancelot, to return again unto this realm and see my tomb and pray some prayer, long or short, for my soul. And this same day that I write this letter I was hurt in the wound that I had from thy hand, Sir Lancelot. By a more noble man might I not be slain.

Also, Sir Lancelot, for all the love that ever was between us, make no tarrying, but come over the sea in all the goodly haste that thou may with thy knights and rescue that noble King who made thee knight, for he is full straitly beset by a false traitor who is my half brother, Sir Mordred.

He went on to write of Mordred's treachery. Then he wet the quill again, with blood from his wound, and continued: *This letter was written but two hours and a half before my death, written with my own hand and subscribed with part of my heart's blood. Therefore I require thee, most famous knight of the world, that thou wilt see my tomb.*

At that point, Gawain sighed and let the quill fall from his hand. He leaned his head against the High King's chest. Arthur signaled for a messenger and gave the letter to him. He waited. From time to time, Gawain spoke, whispering Lancelot's name anxiously, and the High King nodded. At a little past noon, Ar-

As Arthur and Mordred parleyed on the battlefield, a serpent struck a soldier. He drew his sword – a reflex the world would rue.

The gleam of steel teased forth by the serpent brought an instant resumption of battle by the arm

High King and his son. Then hundreds died for Arthur's sake, and hundreds more for Mordred's.

At day's end, the field was a vast charnel house. Mordred lay pierced by his father's spear. Arthur's life

...ing, cut by his son's sword. And only two companions lived to support the High King as he neared the end.

thur lowered Gawain's head to the grass. The gallant heart had failed at last. But the spirit had not failed. The High King's host drove Mordred's armies west, to a great plain that lay not far from the sea. There the two made camp. And Arthur paced through the warm spring night, while the watch fires of Mordred's forces glimmered, small points of light in the rolling dark. At last, he slept. He dreamed then of vipers, the chroniclers said, of a deep pit writhing with serpents; he fell among them and cried out. Startled, the squires who lay on pallets in his tent shook him awake. For the rest of the night, the High King lay watchful while the sentinels called the hour outside and the tethered horses stirred and stamped.

Just before dawn, he sat up, staring. Gawain stood in the tent, stooped and old, a slight smile creasing his face.

"Welcome, sister's son!" the High King cried. "Have you risen from the dead?"

But Gawain shook his head. "If you fight tomorrow, lord, you will die. I know it. You must delay for Lancelot, who will ride from France to you. Make a peace with Mordred. Delay the battle and turn aside fate." He faded from view. Around the floor of the tent, the squires slept on, undisturbed. But Arthur had seen and heard.

So, heartened, the High King thought to alter the pattern of events that he himself had brought about, long years before, when he angered the old ones. At first light, he summoned his warriors and told them of the words the ghost had spoken. He sent his emissaries to Mordred's camp and waited, watching the plain. When they returned, the answer was brief. Mordred would meet with his father on the field. Each man would be attended by fourteen knights only; the armies would stay well back. No weapon would be drawn.

Then, on a late-spring afternoon, when the sun beat down on the battle plain, the great hosts drew into formation. At a herald's cry, the two parties rode out from each line, one under the double eagle and one under the crowns, and Arthur the High King met with his son.

The warriors dismounted in silence, and the two men faced each other. So quiet were they that the creaking of armor and the jingling of harness sounded loud in the field. From a copse of trees a hundred yards away, a cuckoo called once.

"Well, Father," said Mordred, with his narrow smile. Sure of the High King's weakness, he did not bother to conceal contempt. "What have you to offer? That lady the Queen? She has a taste for young men's beds."

A vein beat in the High King's temple, but he would not be drawn. "It is prophesied that you and I will die this day, Mordred, if we do not come to terms," was all he said. It was a wise move. The younger man flinched before his father's level gaze and steady voice; Arthur spoke with power. Then Mordred shrugged, "Well?" he asked again.

"Cornwall and Kent under your rule while I live. All of Britain when I die. You are the son of my body, after all."

Mordred turned to take counsel with his knights. After some moments of whispering, he said, "Done." He grinned and held out his hand to his father.

At that moment, a man cried out. From the corner of his eye, Arthur saw the flash of a striking snake and the steely glitter of a sword as it hissed from the scabbard. For warriors on the verge of battle, their nerves strung tight with apprehension, it needed no more than that. Every sword was drawn; the armies at the edge of the field followed suit, and at once the long, loud cry of the trumpet floated across the grass.

The battle was terrible. Hour after hour, all that afternoon, the armies charged and fell back and charged again. The hordes lost their footing among the bodies on the bloody ground and fell to join the dying. Arthur fought tirelessly, driven by the grief of a man betrayed. The light faded; the charges grew halting, and at last they stopped. Swaying where he stood, the High King surveyed the field, the blindness of his battle fury lifting from his mind.

Far across the western sea, an island fortress floated – the stronghold of the old ones who had woven the fate of the High King.

All around him lay the warriors of the two armies, stripped of dignity in death, their heads split, their faces torn away, their arms reaching stiffly into the air, their hands curled on nothing. Horses lay among them, spilling guts onto the earth. Besides the High King, only three men moved. Two were his own—Bedevere and his brother Lucan, who had fought by his side all the day. They were wounded, but they were alive, and they called his name. Across the field, standing among a heap of twisted corpses, leaning wearily on his sword, stood Mordred, Arthur's son, the evil seed. His face was creased with exhaustion, but he smiled at the High King with a kind of sour triumph.

"Give me my spear," said Arthur to Lucan.

With a company from Faerie, Morgan le Fay sought King Arthur after his last battle and sailed with him into the world of enchantment.

But the knight shook his head. "Sire, we have won the field," he replied. "Leave off now and end this wicked day. Do not tempt fate further, lest you die."

For answer, the King seized a spear that lay among the bodies. He lifted it and, with a shout of rage, assailed his son. Mordred took the point in the belly and staggered back, but he did not fall, nor did he lose his grip on his sword hilt. He fixed his eyes on his father, and step by step, while Arthur stood unmoving, he pushed himself along the spear shaft, until it projected far behind his back and his belly pressed against the hand guard. With deliberation, he swung the broadsword up and brought it down upon the side of Arthur's helmet, so that the blade bit through mail and skull into the brain. Then, still spitted on the spear, he toppled to the earth. The High King's weakening hands released the spear, and he, too, fell.

He lay motionless for long moments, but he was not dead. He opened his eyes when Sir Bedevere bent over him, and he said, "Sir Lucan?"

"Lucan is dying."

"This is my death wound," the High King said. "Carry me to a place where I may hear the sea." When Bedevere lifted him, he fainted, but the labored breathing did not cease. Half carrying him, half dragging, Bedevere bore the High King to a knoll that lay between a small pool of fresh water and the shore, and set him down on the grass underneath a tree. There Arthur rested, eyes closed, while the waves whispered on the strand and dusk faded in the sky. Beside him, Bedevere sat wakeful, watching the moon on the water and listening to the muffled cries and rustlings borne from the battlefield by the night wind.

Presently the King said, "What is the noise?"

"It is the looters," Bedevere replied. "They are robbing the bodies of the warriors and killing any man who breathes. It is always so, after battle." The High King nodded. Then, it seemed, he slept through the night, while Bedevere kept watch.

At first light, Arthur awakened. He gazed at the morning sea and appeared to listen. Then he said, "It is now. Take my broadsword Caliburn and cast it into the pool. It must return to those who forged it." Bedevere unbuckled the sword and walked away with it. When he returned, the High King said, "Tell what you saw."

"Nothing, lord, but wind and wave."

"Bedevere," Arthur replied, "Give my sword into the hands of the old ones."

"It is the sword that made you conqueror and King. Why should we surrender it? I hid it in a safe place."

"Obey me in this last thing," said Arthur. With reluctance, Bedevere left him once more, and once more returned, having seen nothing but wind and wave. The third time he was sent, however, he obeyed the High King's command.

"Lord," he said, and his voice was hushed, "I cast the sword upon the waters. A hand arose from the pool; it grasped the hilt. It brandished Caliburn three times, as if in victory, and then it vanished."

❧ ❧ ❧ ❧ ❧ ❧ ❧ ❧ ❧ ❧ ❧ ❧ ❧ ❧ ❧

And the High King said, "It is well done. See, even now they come for me." That was true. Bedevere gave a gasp of fear and made the sign that averted enchantment. Pacing over the crest of the knoll, their long robes trailing in the grass, their golden crowns gleaming, were three tall women. One had almost the solidity of a mortal, and her features were those of Morgan le Fay. The others trembled in the sunlight, fading in and out of vision; and all around them, more figures shimmered, transparent as dreams. Hands fluttered among the tree branches, clasping gold that might have been the Grail; on the shore, an old man robed in black swayed as if blown by the sea wind. This man had the white beard and long hands of Merlin the Enchanter, and he bowed his head to hear the words of a slender creature that floated beside him.

Morgan kneeled beside the High King. "Brother, the old ones await you," she said. "Now give yourself into their hands, for the fate you set in motion in your youth has completed its course."

Arthur turned his eyes to Bedevere. The look was farewell and command. Helpless to refuse it, the knight lifted the King and bore him down to the sea and placed him on the deck of a small sailing ship that floated there. The ghostly company clustered around the King; a high voice sang in the wind. Then, while Bedevere watched in wonder, the ship turned, as if blown by the very light of morning, and sailed west toward the ancient sea realm of Faerie, where lay an island adorned with apple trees and crowned by a castle of glass.

Bibliography

The Age of Chivalry (The Story of Man Library). Washington, D.C.: National Geographic Society, 1969.

Alcock, Leslie, *Arthur's Britain: History and Archaeology, AD 367-634*. New York: Penguin Books, 1971.

Allen, Douglas, and Douglas Allen Jr., *N. C. Wyeth: The Collected Paintings, Illustrations and Murals*. New York: Bonanza Books, 1972.

Allen, Philip Schuyler, ed., *King Arthur and His Knights: A Noble and Joyous History*. Chicago: Rand McNally, 1924.

Ashe, Geoffrey:
Camelot and the Vision of Albion. London: William Heinemann, 1971.
King Arthur's Avalon: The Story of Glastonbury. London: Collins, 1957.
Ashe, Geoffrey, et al., *The Quest for Arthur's Britain*. London: Granada, 1982.*

Barber, Richard:
King Arthur: In Legend and History. Ipswich, England: Boydell Press, 1973.
The Knight and Chivalry. New York: Harper & Row, 1982.
The Reign of Chivalry. New York: St. Martin's Press, 1980.*

Barber, Richard, comp., *The Arthurian Legends: An Illustrated Anthology*. Totowa, New Jersey: Littlefield Adams, 1979.

Bishop, Morris, *The Horizon Book of the Middle Ages*. New York: American Heritage, 1968.*

Briggs, Katharine M., *Nine Lives: The Folklore of Cats*. New York: Pantheon Books, 1980.*

Bromwich, Rachel, ed. and transl., *Trioedd Ynys Prydein (The Welsh Triads)*. Cardiff, Wales: University of Wales Press, 1961.*

Bruce, James Douglas, *The Evolution of Arthurian Romance: From the Beginnings down to the Year 1300*. Vol. 1. Gloucester, Massachusetts: Peter Smith, 1958 (reprint of 1928 edition).*

Bumke, Joachim, *The Concept of Knighthood in the Middle Ages*. Transl. by W.T.H. Jackson and Erika Jackson. New York: AMS Press, 1982.

Carman, J. Neale, transl., *From Camelot to Joyous Guard: The Old French La Mort le Roi Artu*. Ed. by Norris J. Lacy. Lawrence, Kansas: The University Press of Kansas, 1974.

Castles: A History and Guide. New York: Greenwich House, 1982.

Cavendish, Richard, *King Arthur & the Grail: The Arthurian Legends and Their Meaning*. New York: Taplinger, 1979.*

Cavendish, Richard, ed., *Man, Myth & Magic*. 11 vols. New York: Marshall Cavendish, 1983.*

Chrétien de Troyes, *Arthurian Romances*. Transl. by W. Wistar Comfort. London: J. M. Dent & Sons, 1913.

Cosman, Madeleine Pelner, *Fabulous Feasts: Medieval Cookery and Ceremony*. New York: George Braziller, 1976.

Coulton, G. G., *Medieval Village, Manor, and Monastery*. Gloucester, Massachusetts: Peter Smith, 1975.

Cutts, Edward L., *Scenes and Characters of the Middle Ages*. Detroit: Singing Tree Press, 1968 (reprint of 1872 edition).

Darrah, John, *The Real Camelot: Paganism and the Arthurian Romances*. New York: Thames and Hudson, 1981.

Day, Mildred Leake, ed. and transl., *The Rise of Gawain, Nephew of Arthur* (The Garland Library of Medieval Literature series, Vol. 15). New York: Garland, 1984.

Delort, Robert, *Life in the Middle Ages*. Transl. by Robert Allen. New York: Greenwich House, 1983.*

Ebbutt, M. I., *Hero-Myths & Legends of the British Race*. London: George G. Harrap, 1910.

Evans, J. Gwenogvryn, ed. and transl., *Poems from the Book of Taliesin*. Flanbedrog, Wales: Tremvan, 1915.

Gies, Joseph, and Frances Gies, *Life in a Medieval Castle*. New York: Harper & Row, 1979.

Girouard, Mark, *The Return to Camelot: Chivalry and the English Gentleman*. New Haven, Connecticut: Yale University Press, 1981.

Green, Roger Lancelyn, *King Arthur and His Knights of the Round Table: Newly Re-Told out of the Old Romances*. Harmondsworth, England: Penguin Books, 1982.

Heywood, Thomas, *The Life of Merlin*. London: Lackington, Allen, 1813.

Hibbert, Christopher, *The Search for King Arthur*. New York: American Heritage, 1969.

Hunt, R. W., W. A. Pantin and R. W. Southern, eds., *Studies in Medieval History Presented to Frederick Maurice Powicke*. Westport, Connecticut: Greenwood Press, 1979.

Jackson, Kenneth Hurlstone, *The Gododdin: The Oldest Scottish Poem*. Edinburgh: Edinburgh University Press, 1969.*

Jenkins, Elizabeth, *The Mystery of King Arthur*. New York: Coward, McCann & Geoghegan, 1975.

Karr, Phyllis Ann, *The King Arthur Companion*. Privately published, 1983.*

Keen, Maurice, *Chivalry*. New Haven, Connecticut: Yale University Press, 1984.

Knowles, Sir James, comp., *King Arthur and His Knights*. New York: Harper & Brothers, 1923.

Laing, Lloyd, *Celtic Britain*. London: Granada, 1981.

Lang, Andrew, ed., *The Book of Romance*. London: Longmans, Green, 1902.*

Leach, Maria, ed., *Funk & Wagnalls Standard Dictionary of Folklore, Mythology and Legend*. 2 vols. New York: Funk & Wagnalls, 1949.*

Leathart, Scott, *Trees of the World*. New York: A & W, 1977.

Loomis, Roger Sherman:
The Development of Arthurian Romance. London: Hutchinson, 1963.*
Wales and the Arthurian Legend. Cardiff, Wales: University of Wales Press, 1956.*

Loomis, Roger Sherman, ed., *Arthurian Literature in the Middle Ages*. London: Oxford University Press, 1961.*

Loomis, Roger Sherman, and Laura Hibbard Loomis, *Arthurian Legends in Medieval Art*. London: Oxford University Press, 1938.

Loomis, Roger Sherman, and Laura Hibbard Loomis, eds., *Medieval Romances*. New York: The Modern Library, 1957.

Malory, Sir Thomas:
Le Morte D'Arthur. 2 vols. Ed. by Janet Cowen. New York: Penguin Books, 1982-1983.*
Le Morte Darthur. Ed. by R. M. Lumiansky. New York: Charles Scribner's Sons, 1982.*
Le Morte Darthur: The History of King Arthur and of His Noble Knights of the Round Table. 2 vols. London: Philip Lee Warner for the Medici Society, 1920.*
Tales of King Arthur. Ed. by Michael Senior. New York: Schocken Books, 1981.*

Matthews, William, *The Tragedy of Arthur: A Study of the Alliterative "Morte Arthure."* Berkeley, California: University of California Press, 1960.

Mead, William Edward, *The English Medieval Feast*. London: George Allen & Unwin, 1967.*

Merchant, Elizabeth Lodor, comp., *King Arthur and His Knights*. Chicago: John C. Winston, 1927.

Moncrieff, A. R. Hope, *Romance of Chivalry*. North Hollywood, California: Newcastle Publishing, 1976.

Moorman, Charles, and Ruth Moorman, *An Arthurian Dictionary*. Jackson, Mississippi: University Press of Mississippi, 1978.

Paton, Lucy Allen, *Studies in the Fairy Mythology of Arthurian Romance*. New York: Burt Franklin, 1970 (reprint of 1903 edition).*

Paton, Lucy Allen, transl., *Sir Lancelot of the Lake: A French Prose Romance of the Thirteenth Century*. London: George Routledge & Sons, 1929.*

Platt, Colin, *The Abbeys and Priories of Medieval England*. London: Secker & Warburg, 1984.

Pyle, Howard:
The Story of the Champions of the Round Table. New York: Charles Scribner's Sons, 1933.
The Story of King Arthur and His Knights. New York: Marathon Press, 1978.

Raglan, Lord, *The Hero: A Study in Tradition, Myth, and Drama*. London: Methuen, 1936.

The Reader's Digest Association, ed., *Discovering Britain*. London: Drive Publications, 1982.

Rhys, John, *Studies in the Arthurian Legend*. Oxford, England: Clarendon Press, 1891.

Riordan, James, *Tales of King Arthur*. Chicago: Rand McNally, 1982.

Scudder, Vida D., *Le Morte Darthur of Sir Thomas Malory: A Study of the Book and Its Sources*. New York: Haskell House, 1965.*

Sommer, H. Oskar, ed., *The Vulgate Version of the Arthurian Romances*:
Vol. 2, *Lestoire de Merlin*. New York: AMS Press, 1979 (reprint of 1908-1916 edition).*
Vols. 3, 4 and 5, *Le Livre de Lancelot del Lac*. New York: AMS Press, 1979 (reprint of 1908-1916 editions).*
Vol. 6, *Les Aventures ou la Queste del Saint Graal. La Mort le Roi Artus*. New York: AMS Press, 1969 (reprint of 1913 edition).*
Vol. 7, *Supplement: Le Livre d'Artus*. New York: AMS Press, 1969 (reprint of 1913 and 1916 editions).*

Stephens, Thomas, *The Literature of the Kymry: Being a Critical Essay on the History of the Language and Literature of Wales during the Twelfth and Two Succeeding Centuries*. Ed. by D. Silvan Evans. London: Longmans, Green, 1876.*

Tennyson, Alfred Lord:
The Poems and Plays of Alfred Lord Tennyson. New York: The Modern Library, 1938.*
The Works of Alfred Lord Tennyson. New York: G. P. Putnam's Sons, 1909.

Treharne, R. F., *The Glastonbury Legends: Joseph of Arimathea, The Holy Grail and King Arthur*. London: The Cresset Press, 1967.

Verbruggen, J. F., *The Art of Warfare in Western Europe during the Middle Ages: From the Eighth Century to 1340*. Transl. by Sumner Willard and S. C. M. Southern. Amsterdam: North-Holland, 1977.

Vinaver, Eugene, *The Rise of Romance*. New York: Oxford University Press, 1971.

Wagner, Eduard, *Medieval Costume, Armour and Weapons (1350-1450)*. Transl. by Jean Layton. London: Paul Hamlyn, 1962.*

Warner, Philip, *The Medieval Castle: Life in a Fortress in Peace and War*. London: Arthur Barker, 1971.*

Weston, Jessie L.:
The Legend of Sir Gawain: Studies upon Its Original Scope and Significance. New York: AMS Press, 1972 (reprint of 1897 edition).
The Quest of the Holy Grail. New York: Barnes & Noble, 1964.

Westwood, Jennifer, *Albion: A Guide to Legendary Britain*. London: Granada, 1985.

White, T. H., *The Once and Future King*. New York: Berkley Books, 1983.

Wilcox, R. Turner, *The Mode in Costume*. New York: Charles Scribner's Sons, 1958.*

* Titles marked with an asterisk were especially helpful in the preparation of this volume.

Acknowledgments

The editors wish to thank the following persons and institutions for their help in the preparation of this volume: Ian Ballantine, New York City; Joanna Banham, Whitworth Art Gallery, Manchester, England; A. K. Cooke, King Arthur's Hall Ltd., Tintagel, England; Clark Evans, Rare Book and Special Collections Division, Library of Congress, Washington, D.C.; The Folk-Lore Society, London; Henry Ford, Maas Gallery, London; Phyllis Ann Karr, Rice Lake, Wisconsin; Caroline Krzesinska, Assistant Keeper, Fine Art, Cartwright Hall, Bradford, England; Christine Poulson, London; Jane Revan, Assistant Keeper, Fine Art, Cartwright Hall, Bradford, England; Justin Schiller, New York City; Robert Shields, Rare Book and Special Collections Division, Library of Congress, Washington, D.C.

Picture Credits

The sources for the illustrations in this book are shown below. When it is known, the name of the artist precedes the picture source.

Cover: Artwork by Roberto Innocenti. 1-10: Artwork by Barry Moser. 8-133: Decorative borders by Alicia Austin. 11: William Hatherell, courtesy King Arthur's Hall Ltd., Tintagel, photographed by Derek Bayes, London. 12: Artwork by Michael Hague. 16, 17: Artwork by Barry Moser. 18: Artwork by Troy Howell. 20-22: Artwork by Barry Moser. 24-26: Artwork by Susan Gallagher. 29: Artwork by Barry Moser. 30, 31: Artwork by Gary Kelley. 33: Arthur Rackham from *King Arthur and His Knights of the Round Table*, Macmillan and Co. Ltd., 1917, by permission of Barbara Edwards, courtesy Mary Evans Picture Library, London. 34-39: Artwork by Barry Moser. 40, 41: Artwork by Alan Lee from *Castles* by Alan Lee and David Day, Bantam Books, 1984, New York, photographed by Derek Bayes, London. 43: Artwork by Barry Moser. 44, 45: Artwork by Michael Hague. 47: The Honorable John Collier, courtesy Bradford Art Galleries and Museums. 48: Artwork by Gary Kelley. 50-52: Artwork by Troy Howell. 54-56: Artwork by Barry Moser. 59: W. Russell Flint from *Le Morte d'Arthur* by Sir Thomas Malory, © The Medici Society Ltd., 1910/1911, courtesy Mary Evans Picture Library, London. 60: Artwork by Susan Gallagher. 63: W. Russell Flint from *Le Morte d'Arthur* by Sir Thomas Malory, © The Medici Society Ltd., 1910/1911, courtesy Mary Evans Picture Library, London. 64-69: Artwork by John Howe. 70: Artwork by Barry Moser. 72: Artwork by Gary Kelley. 74-77: Artwork by Barry Moser. 78, 79: Artwork by Yvonne Gilbert. 80: W. Russell Flint from *Le Morte d'Arthur* by Sir Thomas Malory, © The Medici Society Ltd., 1910/1911, courtesy Mary Evans Picture Library, London. 82-86: Artwork by Barry Moser. 87: Artwork by Yvonne Gilbert. 88: W. Russell Flint from *Le Morte d'Arthur* by Sir Thomas Malory, © The Medici Society Ltd., 1910/1911, courtesy Mary Evans Picture Library, London. 90-93: Artwork by Barry Moser. 94, 95: Artwork by Troy Howell. 96: Artwork by Barry Moser. 98: Artwork by Michael Hague. 100: Artwork by Barry Moser. 101: H. J. Ford from *The Book of Romance* by Andrew Lang, copyright Longmans Ltd., 1917, courtesy The British Library, London. 102: Artwork by Susan Gallagher. 105-109: Artwork by Michael Hague. 110: Artwork by Barry Moser. 112, 113: Artwork by John Howe. 115: H. J. Ford from *The Book of Romance* by Andrew Lang, copyright Longmans Ltd., 1917, courtesy The British Library, London. 116: William Hatherell, courtesy King Arthur's Hall Ltd., Tintagel, photographed by Derek Bayes, London. 118-123: Artwork by Barry Moser. 124: Artwork by Yvonne Gilbert. 126, 127: Artwork by Gary Kelley. 129-133: Artwork by John Howe. 135: Artwork by Barry Moser. 136, 137: J. G. Archer, Manchester City Art Gallery, courtesy The Bridgeman Art Library, London. 139-144: Artwork by Barry Moser.

Chief Series Consultant

Tristram Potter Coffin, Professor of
English at the University of Pennsylvania, is a leading authority on folklore.
He is the author or editor of numerous
books and more than one hundred articles. His best-known works are *The British Traditional Ballad in North America, The
Old Ball Game, The Book of Christmas Folklore* and *The Female Hero.*

This volume is one of a series that is based
on myths, legends and folk tales.

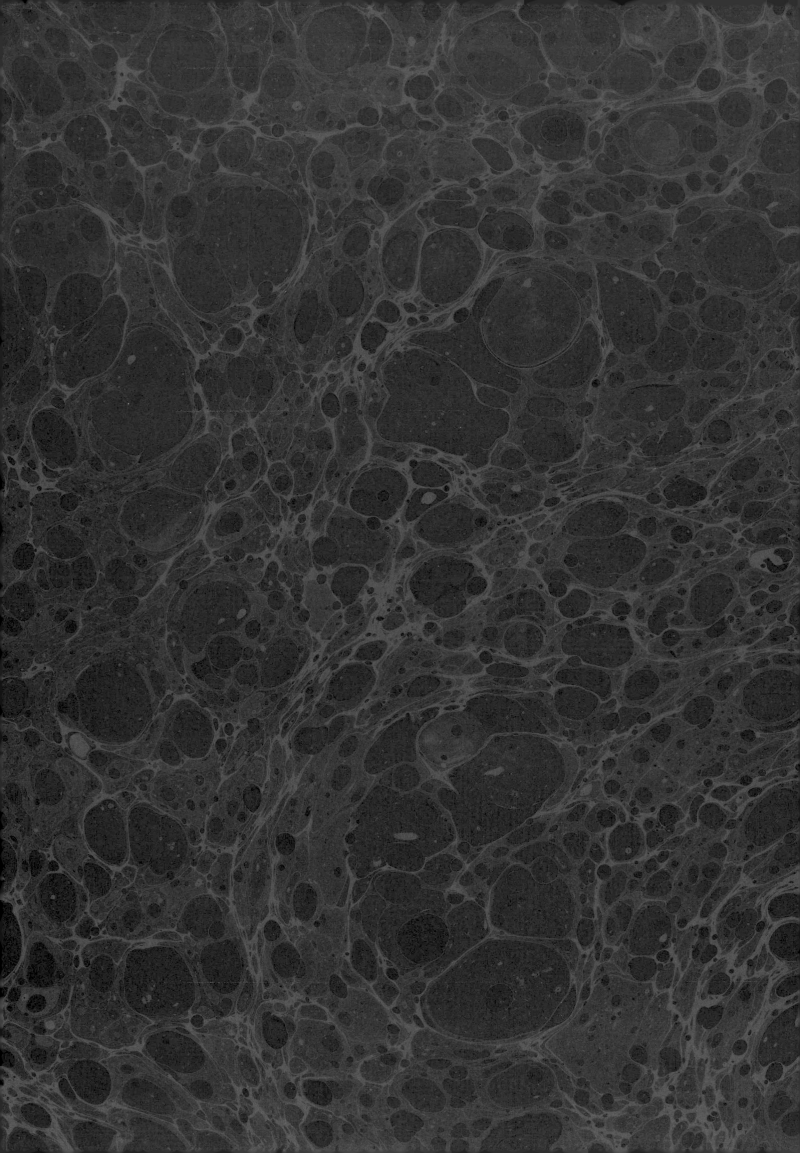